LIFE WITH FLOWERS

FRANCES PALMER
LIFE WITH FLOWERS

INSPIRATION AND LESSONS FROM THE GARDEN

FOREWORD BY ERIN BENZAKEIN

ARTISAN | NEW YORK

Library of Congress Cataloging-in-Publication Data is on file.

ISBN 978-1-64829-139-5

Design by Jane Treuhaft and Elizabeth Van Itallie

Published by Artisan, an imprint of Workman Publishing, a division of Hachette Book Group, Inc. 1290 Avenue of the Americas New York, NY 10104 artisanbooks.com

The Artisan name and logo are registered trademarks of Hachette Book Group, Inc.

Printed in China on responsibly sourced paper

First printing, March 2025

10 9 8 7 6 5 4 3 2 1

TO MY FAMILY

CONTENTS

Foreword 9

Introduction 11

My Approach to Cutting Gardens 14

Inspirations from the Garden World 21

PART I
PREVERNAL

Hellebores 26

Snowdrops and Crocuses 29

Fritillaries 33

Early-Flowering Branches 36

Muscaris 43

Daffodils 44

Flowers Make the Best Gifts 48

Hyacinths 51

Auriculas 55

PART II
VERNAL

Lilacs 61

Flower-Topped Sugar Cookies 62

Tulips 64

Photography and Flowers Go Hand in Hand 71

Making Flower Anthotypes 75

Peonies 79

Azaleas 83

Bearded Irises 87

Dogwoods and Viburnums 92

Lilies of the Valley 96

Bleeding Hearts 99

Leaving a Garden in Bloom 100

Roses 102

Quince Jelly with Rose Petals 111

PART III
AESTIVAL

Poppies 114

Flowering Vines and Climbers 120

Lentil Salad with Nasturtiums 128

Lilies 131

Fantastic Spires 137

Flowering Herbs 144

Halibut with Chives in Parchment 152

PART IV

SEROTINAL

Hydrangeas 156

Gladioli 159

The Camaraderie of Flower Growers 163

Sunflowers 164

I Do My Best Thinking in the Garden 169

Echinaceas and Rudbeckias 170

Cosmos 176

Marigolds 179

Risotto with Fresh Flowers 180

Making Marigold-Dyed Napkins 183

Zinnias 187

Leaves That I Love 191

PART V

AUTUMNAL

Dahlias 199

The Beauty in the Chaos 209

Chrysanthemums 210

Pollinator Species 214

Asters 223

Amaranths 224

Japanese Anemones 228

Making Pressed-Flower Cards 232

PART VI

HIBERNAL

Holiday Flowers 236

Dreaming of the Garden in Bloom 242

Pelargoniums and Geraniums 245

Rose Geranium Pound Cake 248

Greenhouse Flowers 250

Orchids 258

Best Practices for Buying Flowers 262

GROWING YOUR OWN

Flower Growing Basics 268

Flower Arranging Basics 276

Gardens to Visit 278

Go-To Suppliers 280

Further Reading 282

Acknowledgments 283

Index 284

FOREWORD

I first met Frances Palmer in the spring of 2015, when she came to our farm to attend a seasonal floral design workshop. I had long admired her work from afar, so when I saw her name show up on the student roster, I went into a full-fledged panic. What on earth could she possibly have to learn from me? Frances was, after all, a renowned and established artist, a savvy businesswoman, and an incredibly talented floral designer in her own right. I, on the other hand, was a budding floral designer, and Floret was just starting to find success.

But after meeting Frances, I realized that my nerves were unnecessary. She was (and remains) one of the most generous, warm, and down-to-earth people I've ever met, instantly putting me and the other attendees at ease. We spent three flower-filled days together talking about business, creativity, valuing your work and yourself—all while harvesting truckloads of flowers from our fields and making glorious arrangements. And it just so happened that the peonies, one of Frances's favorite flowers, were in peak bloom. It was so much fun to watch her discover varieties she hadn't seen before, and her excitement about them was contagious.

In the years that followed we've stayed in touch, and Frances has been a sounding board during pivotal times in my career. I distinctly remember the day she took me out to lunch in New York City before a big event where we were both speakers. At that time, I was under a tremendous amount of pressure to scale our business, with so many saying bigger was better. Frances, always the voice of reason, asked me what I really wanted out of life and encouraged me to follow my own path, define success on my own terms, and be true to myself. Looking back, those words have been a North Star over the last decade and really helped me to stay the course.

And that course begins and ends with flowers. As Frances writes in her introduction, I, too, integrate them into all aspects of my life. And while I've been working with them for twenty years now, this book offered me an entirely new perspective and a whole world of information I had yet to learn. I discovered cultivars I hadn't heard of before, learned about her treasured sources for plants, and picked up special growing tricks that Frances has developed over her many decades as a gardener. Each group of plants profiled includes their rich history, a list of her must-grow varieties, plus tips for how to arrange with them—it's the perfect balance of information and inspiration. Most of all, I love seeing the flowers through Frances's eyes and witnessing how her deep appreciation for the natural world inspires her other creative pursuits, and vice versa.

If you're a gardener or a flower lover, be forewarned: Your garden will inevitably expand after reading this book. But the real gift is the wisdom you'll find in these pages. We all have something to learn from Frances.

—ERIN BENZAKEIN
Founder of Floret Flower Farm

INTRODUCTION

As a potter, I have spent nearly four decades producing ceramic pieces for everyday life. In that time, growing and arranging flowers has served as a parallel practice to my work in the studio. Together, the unyielding clay and the flowering plants, each fragile and temperamental, form a bond that is central to both endeavors. I consider the pottery and the flowers as the two halves of my earthly paradise.

Not long after I began designing and creating pots, I started to display flowers within them. What I've found is that the flowers and the pots exist in a symbiotic relationship. I honestly can't imagine one without the other. Each morning throughout the long growing seasons, I bring cut flowers or branches into the studio to arrange in the pots. As I walk around the garden beds or among the flowering shrubs and trees just beyond them, I consider how the flowers in bloom will work in conjunction with the vessels. Sometimes I choose the flower to fit the pot I have in mind; other times I work in reverse.

Making ceramics and growing flowers require me to work with my hands, using elements of the earth, and to be receptive to what the material has to say. Each of these pursuits delivers dynamic contrast to the other, while both keep me continually delighted and engaged.

Despite all best efforts, multiple variables exist beyond my control. The garden is influenced by the weather, the health of the soil, and my ability and willingness to care for it, while the formation of the pots depends on my hands and what transpires in the firing environment of the kiln. In each case, I remain open to the outcome, which can vary greatly between the generally predicted and the wildly unexpected. There is satisfaction in the result in either instance, and I never tire of the element of surprise.

I recognize that pairing flowers with pottery is nothing new. Since ancient times, gardeners have used terra-cotta— a readily available clay body—with flowers. In my ongoing research into the history of pottery, I love to study the shapes of vases and countless other clay vessels through history, most often at the Metropolitan Museum of Art in New York City and also in my travels. A couple of years ago, I visited the exhibition *Grounded in Clay* at the Museum of Indian Arts and Culture in Sante Fe, New Mexico. Reading the catalog gave me a new appreciation for the Pueblo Indian pottery tradition and the importance of water and nature in their practice. Acknowledging the art form that has been passed down through multiple generations, the potters thank the earth for the clay that they dig and the sacred water that is used to make the pots. They articulate a reverence that I also feel. I thank the earth and strive to keep it healthy and vibrant as it helps me express the ideas in my head in physical form.

In the studio and in the garden, I embrace going slowly and aim to take the long view. Just as my ceramics practice has deepened in ways I could never have foreseen thirty-eight years ago, the garden is an ever-evolving project. I continually seek out the plants that will be happiest here and will produce the most intriguing flowers to showcase in the pots.

This book is a study in how I integrate flowers into all aspects of my life—the garden, the pottery studio, our house, my travels—all year round. On the pages that follow, I describe in detail why I am inspired to grow the flowers I choose to plant, from popular favorites like peonies and dahlias to lesser-known bleeding hearts and amaranths, as well as the flowering trees of spring, herbs, pollinators, and the blooms I cultivate indoors. Throughout, I offer the best practices I've learned from years of cultivating and arranging these plants.

The chapters are loosely arranged to follow the flowers as they appear in my Connecticut garden. Rather than the four seasons of the conventional calendar—winter, spring, summer, and fall—the book is divided into six periods of growth according to a botanical calendar—prevernal, vernal, aestival, serotinal, autumnal, and hibernal. Because there's a rhythm to the natural order of plants, I prefer to think of the flowers in terms of waves rather than specific seasons or months in the year. I envision their bloom times as a series of occurrences that ebb and flow from one into the next. Beginning with the very earliest delicate buds in late February and early March and proceeding all the way through the glorious peak-season peonies to the hardy chrysanthemums in November, just before the frost arrives, each variety of flower completes its cycle in its own time. As one finishes, another is about to open or is already at its midway point, like a ballet where dancers glide on and off the stage.

As many authors have written, gardens feed the soul and give a visitor an emotional and physical respite. Many a time when stressed I have walked out of my studio into the garden to calm and balance myself. The beauty of the flowers is a daily gift that can't be quantified, and I marvel at each unique bud.

The first waves of growth in the garden offer an exuberant range of colors and shapes. When the species tulips and delicate daffodils appear, I gather a bunch and place them in a varied group of vases in my studio, where they deliver instant cheer.

My Approach to Cutting Gardens

When I was growing up, my mother made a small garden in the backyard of our home in Morristown, New Jersey. It was nothing fancy—mainly peonies in spring, zinnias and tomatoes in summer—but it fulfilled her needs. My first true vision of how magical a garden could be was inspired by Sir John Tenniel's illustration of Alice talking to the tiger lily in the Garden of Live Flowers, from Lewis Carroll's *Through the Looking-Glass*, which I reread often. It seemed perfectly natural to me for Alice

Alice and the Tiger Lily from *Through the Looking-Glass*, Sir John Tenniel, 1871.

to be pictured in conversation with the different flowers. I, too, have conversed with flowers all my life. Each flower type has its own persona, as Tenniel captured so well. I think of these possible dialogues when I design my arrangements, imagining the tête-à-tête that the flowers are having together in the garden bed they share, and later, how they will coexist in the vase.

During my twenties, when I lived in New York City, I made a weekly trip to the Twenty-Eighth Street flower market, where I bought tulips, roses, and lilies as they became available. I especially loved anything with a strong scent, including 'Casa Blanca' lilies. In my apartment, there was always something on display in a vase. But it wasn't until my family moved to Connecticut that I was able to begin my life as a gardener.

After the birth of my daughter (the oldest of my three children) in 1986, my husband, Wally, and I moved to a mid-century house in Weston. I began my pottery practice around the same time and made my first forays into gardening. It was a period of great exploration and growth for me, on many levels.

When our needs for space for the children and my budding ceramics business outgrew our family's first house, we moved across town. Beyond the house itself, what attracted me to our new home was the open, flat land that surrounded it, which would allow me to fulfill my dream of having a true cutting garden. There was an existing, unfenced, pie-wedged plot of mostly daylilies that were routinely eaten by deer. After trying to work with these beds for a year or two, it was clear that we needed to protect the plants from the local wildlife. To keep the animals out, Wally and I constructed a simple fence that created a 50-foot (15 m) diameter round garden. We devised a 16-square-foot (5 sq m) bed design with paths in between, leaving smaller sections around the perimeter against the fence. The round garden was not glamorous, but it greatly increased the square footage from the original layout and allowed for flowers, including tulips and dahlias, to be planted in rows.

Several years later, when my flower fixation was approaching critical mass, we converted an unused tennis court on the property into a second cutting garden. There I've been happily growing all manner of flowering plants ever since, in thirty raised beds. It's also where I keep four beehives, whose residents pollinate the flowers and herbs and everything else that thrives in the garden.

More recently, I realized another long-held dream: In 2019, we built a greenhouse off the back of the studio basement. There I cultivate plants that cannot survive the winter temperatures before moving them outside once it gets warmer.

I never set out to have a formal garden but rather intended to create a hardworking plot that exists as a sibling to my studio. I embrace the unpredictability that ensues once I sow a seed or plant a plug anywhere within the teeming landscape. The same flower may bloom in the same spot from one year to the next, or it may surprise me by appearing elsewhere as a volunteer. I'm delighted either way.

The mission for my planting plan is clear: to stagger the ongoing display so that it provides constant and uninterrupted flowers in a continual flow of colors, heights, and shapes for arranging in my pottery. Ideally, there's not a single moment from early March until late November when something is not in bloom. To achieve the fullest range, I start by considering which plants open at which times, and when possible, within each family of flowers, the varieties that peak early, middle, and late in the bloom cycle. This information is usually included in the catalog entry for each bulb or seed. Beyond that, much of the knowledge I've acquired about bloom times comes from personal observation in the garden over many growing seasons. From earliest springtime until the first frost, I walk out to the garden to check what is about to open, in full bloom, or beginning to fade, and then decide what is best to cut.

As a result, I've developed a garden plan that I rely on year after year. It's

Following spread: Throughout the growing season (from early March to late November), I try to walk in the round garden each day to see what needs to be addressed and to simply take in the beauty of the flowers.

a working list of what I hope to have available in the beds for cutting and photographing over the course of many months. Within each perennial flower family, I include a range of colors, shapes, and textures, which allows for the greatest stock of plant material to work with and lends a beautiful diversity to the garden and the arrangements. I also add annuals and flowering shrubs that I find at plant sales and nurseries. And increasingly, I'm planting lots of pollinators throughout both cutting gardens, as I now understand how important a balance in the garden is for the ongoing health of the environment. During the winter months, my approach is more restrained, and I am forced to use what is blooming in the greenhouse or to call upon a houseplant or flowers that I have purchased to contribute to an arrangement.

Though the flowers I grow must fulfill their function in a pot, I marvel at their beauty in the garden beds. I order myself to cut the most beautiful blooms and not allow their perfection to keep me from using them in arrangements and immortalizing them in photographs. Annuals are especially valuable in this endeavor, as their blooms will keep opening even after they are cut. In fact, the cutting is what encourages new flowers to form.

My ongoing experimentation requires patience and perseverance, in equal measure. After all, growing flowers is not a strictly linear process. It's taken much trial and error to discover which flowers work well in my garden; and the weather, which fluctuates from year to year, influences my success (as it does for any gardener, regardless of experience or training). I remain open to the challenges and opportunities, all the while aware that every growing season is different. In fact, that unpredictable nature of the process is what keeps me engaged and determined to keep going.

This photo of the raised beds on the tennis court was taken in 2014, before I installed drip irrigation pipes and added rosebushes in pots down the length of the garden. The area looks less neat today. I no longer grow vegetables, preferring to give all the space to flowers.

Inspirations from the Garden World

My garden is influenced by many different experiences, whether firsthand (in-person visits) or from afar (books, mainly). From the beginning, I have sought to learn from the garden masters—many of them British, as I share a sensibility with their garden philosophy and because we can grow most of the same flowers here in Connecticut, though usually a month or two later on the calendar.

The English artist Vanessa Bell is at the top of my list of garden heroes. In 1916, when she was in her mid-thirties, she moved to a farmhouse known as Charleston with her partner, the painter Duncan Grant. Both were part of the Bloomsbury group of artists who maintained a free and creative lifestyle as an act of rebellion against England's Victorian morality. When I started making ceramics and planting flowers, Charleston was my inspiration. Bell kept her garden just outside her studio and at the most manageable size. Originally it was used to grow produce, but presently it is mainly filled with perennials, annuals, and fruit trees. Charleston is now a museum with wonderful exhibitions and events, and I have visited it numerous times.

I am also completely bowled over and inspired by the borders at the Great Dixter Charitable Trust in Northiam,

East Sussex, England, created by its founding gardener, Christopher Lloyd. The Victorian architect Edwin Lutyens originally designed the garden layout, but when Lloyd inherited the property in 1954, he transformed it into one of the great English gardens and plant nurseries. He was an avid garden writer who published twenty-five books and had a weekly column in *Country Life* magazine for forty-two years. Lloyd's love for color is evident in the different garden rooms at Great Dixter, which feature exquisite plant combinations. "The borders are mixed, not herbaceous," he wrote. "I see no point in segregating plants of differing habit or habits. They can all help one another. So, you'll see shrubs, climbers, hardy and tender perennials, annuals and biennials, all growing together and contributing to the overall tapestry." That is the magic of the place.

Opposite: The ever-changing long border at Great Dixter, with Christopher Lloyd's family home in the background.

Below: A glimpse of the Charleston farmhouse from the back of the garden with the dahlias and fruit trees in full splendor. The windows of Vanessa Bell's studio are seen in the distance.

The cupboard at my friend Charlie McCormick's flower room in his former home in Dorset held the most wonderful display of his collection of Constance Spry's Fulham Pottery vessels. These pieces were designed and produced from the 1930s through the 1950s to hold Constance's eclectic flower arrangements and are highly prized today.

Fergus Garrett joined Christopher Lloyd as head gardener of Great Dixter in 1993 and worked with him until Lloyd's death in 2006. He is currently the brilliant steward and chief executive of the trust, training a generation of plantspeople who have gone on to manage gardens around the planet. Garrett lectures and educates continually, examining best growing practices and biodiversity for our changing environment. I have learned so much from his talks about plants and how he navigates garden trends such as wilding and native proponents. I had the good fortune to stay at Great Dixter in September 2023 and could wander around the garden in the mornings as the sun was rising. I was thrilled to see many of the same flowers—such as amaranth, rudbeckia, salvia, and dahlia—that are in my gardens, although my raised beds are on a minute scale in comparison.

I often reference Constance Spry, a British floral designer who lived from 1886 until 1960, when I am in the garden looking for flowers to arrange.

Spry had a garden wherever she lived and was extremely knowledgeable about the plant world. She significantly changed how flowers were perceived and used in arrangements at the time, because she considered all growing things useful for arranging: vegetables, hedgerow plants, weeds from the roadside, tree branches and leaves, and, of course, flowers. Friends noticed her unusual displays and asked her to make similar designs for them. Her first flower shop evolved over time into a global business. From the 1930s onward, she became the go-to person for high-society events, the pinnacle being the floral extravaganza for Queen Elizabeth II's coronation in 1953. Spry wrote numerous books on flower decoration as well as cookery to inspire readers to broaden their ideas about what could be considered beautiful in a vase and to encourage them to cook from their gardens. Spry remains a huge influence on designers today.

My admiration of Cedric Morris is twofold: He was a celebrated painter as well as a plantsman. Morris was known for breeding highly prized bearded iris varieties (designated by the 'Benton' prefix). I've been inspired by him since I saw an exhibition of his flower and vegetable paintings at the Garden Museum in London in 2018 (and have been on an ongoing quest to add more bearded irises to my own garden). He and his partner, Arthur Lett-Haines, opened the East Anglian School of Painting and Drawing in 1939, in the farmhouse called Benton End in Suffolk. At their unconventional school, students were urged to take their canvases outside and develop a painting style on their own. By design, there was not a lot of teacher instruction (for that reason I would have loved to study there!). Morris painted his flowers exquisitely. I especially love *Iris Seedlings* (see page 87) from 1943, now at the Tate Gallery in London. He brought back rare flower bulbs from his trips to Turkey and the Mediterranean during the winter months and planted them at Benton End, which is now under the auspices of the Garden Museum. The farmhouse and gardens are currently being restored, and I eagerly look forward to visiting when they are reopened.

An archival image of Cedric Morris's iris beds in his garden at Benton End taken circa 1946/7 by *Country Life*'s longtime gardens editor Tony Venison. Morris was a renowned breeder of exquisite irises, and his varieties have now been revived. The garden is also under restoration, with the ghosts of his flowers reappearing.

PART I

PREVERNAL

AFTER THE WINTER SOLSTICE IN DECEMBER, EACH day stays lighter for a bit longer in the morning and afternoon, until the summer solstice in June. In the prevernal period (roughly from late February/early March until the last days of April, depending on where you live), buds begin to appear on tree branches and tiny green leaves start to sprout, sometimes through snow. Birds return, bringing welcome sights and sounds after winter's long gray stillness. Emerging during the deep thaw, we humans are rewarded for the time we spent nesting indoors, patiently watching and waiting, planning and plotting out the days to come in the garden.

At this time of year, I order the flower plugs that I will plant once the soil warms as well as the organic cow manure to spread over the garden beds. I prune the rosebushes and cut back the perennial stalks and stems that were left for the insects in winter so that spring's fresh growth can come through uninhibited. And then one day, seemingly from out of nowhere, up spring the hellebores, followed in short order by the indefatigable daffodils and the funkily fragrant hyacinths. Admittedly, though, this season can be a bit cruel. The tiniest harbingers of the season may trick us into thinking we are in the clear, until a cold snap reminds us that there are still some weeks to pass before the garden is on its way to full bloom.

Hellebores

I've long admired hellebores, which are often the first plants to emerge out of the cold ground here in Connecticut. After observing the wide variety of hellebore plants growing in wonderful clumps in Sakonnet Garden in Little Compton, Rhode Island, designed by my friends Mikel Folcarelli and John Gwynne, I ordered from the supplier they suggested (Pine Knot Farms). These plants will bloom profusely as long as they are happy in their growing spot (all varieties like moist soil and dappled shade). In my round garden, I've had two *Helleborus niger* with large creamy white flowers for many seasons. The flowers bloom intermittently, even beneath the snow. The previous few seasons, I have been experimenting to find new places to plant them. I put in several later-blooming types on the north side of the greenhouse, where they performed well last spring; the leaves look large and healthy this year.

The genus *Helleborus* contains over twenty species, including the aforementioned *H. niger* (commonly called Christmas rose, because it blooms in early December) and *H. orientalis* (or Lenten rose, which blooms in early spring). They are all herbaceous perennials and members of the Ranunculaceae family. They are also poisonous; the word *helleborus* is a combination of the Greek *heleîn*—"to injure"—and *borá*, meaning "food." As a result, animals steer clear of hellebores, so you don't have to be too cautious about where you plant them; there's no need to hide them behind a garden fence.

Hellebores are available in a variety of colors: black, white, mauve, peach, and pale green. In the early-winter months, the plants can be found in some specialty supermarkets and flower shops. They make great potted plants for indoor displays and are easy to transplant into the ground post–bloom time. Select potted hellebores in full bloom so you know what their flowers will look like in the garden.

These graceful flowers are beautiful and unexpected in arrangements all by themselves or combined with other early bloomers such as muscaris and daffodils, as well as with witch hazel branches. Some people cut out the center stamens for a cleaner look and longer life in the vase, but I do not, as I feel that doing so mars the beauty of the bloom. If the stems of your cut hellebores droop in the vase, put the whole flower in a bowl or bucket of cold water overnight and they should resaturate. You can also put a pinhole through the stem, which facilitates its absorbing water.

A freshly cut bunch of hellebores in a range of colors makes an especially cheerful display when the garden is still mostly dormant. The painted cobalt details in this porcelain vase echo the speckles in the flower petals.

Snowdrops and Crocuses

January, February, and early March in Connecticut can be dark and dreary, with weeks on end of gray sky and gray ground. I realize that the cold and snow are essential to the trees, bulbs, and perennials of this climate, so I am accepting of the predicament and try to remain patient. When the snowdrops appear, with the crocuses in quick succession, it feels like we are in the homestretch and that spring is not too far away.

Neither snowdrops nor crocuses come to mind when we think of cut flowers, and I generally don't use either of them in mixed arrangements. Nonetheless, I have found ways to bring their beauty indoors as I wait for the sturdier flowers to come into bloom in my cutting gardens.

Both are lovely in the smallest bud vases placed on a bathroom sink or bedside table; you don't need many to make an impact. Sometimes I dig up a clump of either flower, surrounding soil and all, and set it in a bowl to display on the dining table. Once the blooms start to fade, I gather up the clump and return it outside, back into the hole from which it was dug. The bulbs (or corms) resituate themselves, and the flowers return the following year, right on time.

You can also force crocus bulbs, which are available for sale in early fall from bulb suppliers, nurseries, and home centers (see page 271 for instructions). Having bulbs in bloom inside the house and the studio helps brighten up the dull gray days of January and February. And to have something that is truly from the garden is the perfect segue out of the last dark winter days into the light of spring.

(see page 271 for instructions).

Opposite and below: A large clump of snowdrops, lifted from my garden with their roots still attached, look right at home in a blue celadon bowl. I like how the textural bumps on the piece (made with my fingertips when the clay was thrown) mimic the delicate heads of the flowers.

Below and opposite:
The intense purple of
the crocus that has
naturalized in our
yard is astounding in
contrast to the mostly
frozen brown earth.
When brought indoors,
the bulbs are held in
place in a shallow
bowl; I am careful to
keep the soil moist
without overwatering.

SNOWDROP

In recent years, there has been a great deal of interest in the delicate galanthus, more commonly known as the snowdrop. Galanthus societies abound, including one that hosts a Galanthus Gala every spring. The bulbs can be easily sourced from garden catalogs and planted in fall before the ground freezes solid; this is usually on my October to-do list, depending on the weather.

Once planted, snowdrops return reliably and often spread, especially under trees. They don't have a strong scent, but they are small, cheery harbingers of spring, often coming into bloom beneath a blanket of snow (hence their name).

CROCUS

Exuberant purple crocuses with gorgeous orange stamens crop up all around our yard each year, usually well before the middle of March. I love to see the pops of color bursting forth from beneath leaves. The flowers predate my arrival at the house, but they appear to be *Crocus tommasinianus* 'Ruby Giant'. Crocuses are one of the easiest bulbs (or corms) to force and grow indoors in pots; in fall, when all the spring-blooming flower bulbs are shipped, I try to reserve a few of the crocuses for forcing (see page 271).

In the ground, crocuses thrive in full sun, though partial shade is fine. They are especially impactful when planted in clusters in lawns and within garden beds beneath trees, where they create a colorful drift in the slowly emerging landscape of late winter/early spring. Plant them in autumn, well before the first hard frost (crocus, like all fall-planted spring bulbs or corms, needs a period of winter dormancy to bloom in spring). The ideal soil is moist but well drained, to prevent rot. Another bonus of crocus plants is that they attract pollinators; the bees are enthralled by their stamens. Once they've flowered, let them die back completely, and they should return the next year. Crocuses are not technically deer- and rodent-proof, but mine have never been eaten, mercifully.

Fritillaries

Every fall I plant fritillaries, crossing my fingers that they will bloom in the garden several months later. I am constantly thrilled by their bell-shaped florets and their coloring. Most years they deliver, but if they don't bloom, it's a sign that I should lift the bulbs and replant them more shallowly. I was just reading that they like to be planted right after shipping in fall, but I often leave the bulbs in the boxes for a few weeks before I have time to put them in the beds, and perhaps that's a factor for the bloomless years—I haven't allowed enough time for roots to develop before the hard frosts come. Further complicating matters, the evil voles manage to get into the beds in winter and eat the bulbs. Some people plant the bulbs in chicken-wire cages for this reason, but I never find enough time to do so. Ultimately, I just keep replanting and hope for the best.

When my order arrives, I can immediately smell the pungent, musky bags of fritillary bulbs, which explains the fact that the flowers are also known as "stink" or "skunk" lilies. Once the fritillaries emerge from the soil, I can smell them on the tennis court beds from yards away. I love this malodorous perfume, which stays with the flowers once cut and placed in a vase. Some people object, but I find it fascinating.

Fritillaries originated in the Himalayas and Asia Minor. Here in Connecticut, I plant three sizes of these perennials, which are part of the lily family (Liliaceae). The largest, *Fritillaria imperialis* 'Rubra Maxima' (also known as crown imperial), is incredibly majestic, with up to ten bright orange or yellow flowers per stem and a deep garnet lining underneath (and one of the strongest scents of all). Next, I plant the deeply elegant *F. persica* (often called Persian lily), a dark, blue-black color with tiny yellow centers within the hanging bell-shaped blooms. Finally, I can't get enough of the *F. meleagris*, a tiny miracle of a flower with the most magnificent checkerboard pattern. No matter how often I see one of these fritillaries in bloom, I never fail to wonder how it is so perfectly created, and I increase the number I plant the following season, just to make sure I have enough to cut and admire indoors.

I look forward to seeing fritillaries in the garden, among the hyacinths and muscaris, but their real value for me is in the vase, where they make an unexpected addition to mixed arrangements. I often pair them with early tulips and daffodils. When displayed all by themselves, however, their delicate details shine. *F. meleagris* works especially well in photographs.

To get a small jump on seeing fritillaries ahead of their usual bloom time, I sometimes force the bulbs (and others, including muscaris) in pots in the greenhouse. This allows me to examine the extraordinary checkerboard pattern of the *Fritillaria meleagris* variety at close range.

An exhibition of my wood-fired pottery offered a great opportunity to display the fritillaries growing on the tennis court. Included in the mix are *Fritillaria imperialis* 'Rubra Maxima' and 'Maxima Lutea', *F. meleagris* and *F. meleagris* var. *unicolor* subvar. *alba*, as well as *F. persica*.

Early-Flowering Branches

Pussy Willow, Witch Hazel, Forsythia, Magnolia, Redbud, and Blossoming Fruit Trees

While late winter morphs into the prevernal period, several trees and bushes begin blossoming outside my window. As I write this, on the first day of February, the buds on the shrubs that surround my studio look promising. The pussy willow is blooming, and the witch hazel is just beginning to open. But there is still a long way to go until garden flowers return in earnest in late March.

In the meantime, forced branches are a lovely way to bring a few blossoms into the home a bit ahead of the weather. The flowering branches lift the spirits because they hint at what is still to come in the landscape. I am careful to take branches in a way that will not compromise the balance of the tree or shrub when it eventually comes into full bloom. Once the branches are placed into vases filled with warm water, the flowers will gradually open and last for weeks indoors.

PUSSY WILLOW

With its downy pendulum flowers, the pussy willow shrub (genus *Salix*) is an early magnet for bees of all kinds. Where I live, that means the bumblebees, honeybees, and sand wasps. On especially warm spring days, when the pussy willow in my garden is covered with the buzzing insects, I can see mounds of pollen stored on their hind legs as they head back to their hives. Since the willow thrives in moist soil, I planted one in the swale; this low spot on the property is usually damp and becomes a temporary river after heavy spring rains. The shrub appears to be happy there, as it has since grown very large.

When cut and brought inside, the branches' silver shimmer is cheerful in a vase, offering a tactile comfort. I like to display large bunches in tall vases on their own or cut the branches very short and use them as underpinnings to support daffodils and other early bloomers in an arrangement. If left long enough in the water, the branches will root, and can then be transplanted easily into a pot or directly into the garden.

WITCH HAZEL

About a decade ago, I was introduced to Japanese witch hazel (*Hamamelis japonica*)

A metal flower frog keeps flowering branches upright in a widemouthed vessel. For these witch hazel branches, I chose a shino-glazed dark stoneware bowl, which works well with the brown branches and ethereal yellow petals.

Border forsythia
Apple
American pussy willow

Eastern redbud
Star magnolia
Japanese witch hazel

Yulan/lily magnolia
'Jelena' witch hazel
Apricot

on an early-spring visit to Wave Hill, the beautiful 28-acre (11.3 ha) public garden that overlooks the Hudson River, in the northwest corner of the Bronx. I was thrilled to see that the plant was already blooming, and I resolved to cultivate one at home. At Broken Arrow Nursery in Hamden, Connecticut, I found a similar witch hazel with yellow flowers, and a winter hazel (*Corylopsis*), a bush in the witch hazel family. Last May I also planted the red-blossomed hybrid *Hamamelis* × *intermedia* 'Jelena', which grows more quickly than other varieties. All three bloom roughly around the same time. I especially love the petals of the winter hazel, which form small, drooping clusters producing numerous branches and buds.

Witch hazels are generally slow growers, so patience is definitely in order. They perform well with pruning every couple of years. Now that my plants are established, I cut the branches sparingly to encourage full and even growth. The small, ribbonlike flowers have a lovely, fresh citrusy scent that permeates a room.

Once the flowers begin to fade, a handful can be gathered with a tablespoon of bark, chopped up, boiled in a cup of water for 30 minutes, then strained to create a tincture for dry skin and rashes. I also save the pruned branches, which can be used as excellent trellises for sweet peas planted outside in pots or as supports for indoor potted orchids.

FORSYTHIA

Over the years, I've heard forsythia dismissed by some horticulturists as plebeian and unworthy of serious attention, but I wholeheartedly disagree. In fact, I consider it to be one of the great unsung heroes of the garden. Every April, without fail, the bright yellow forsythia in our yard serves as a much-needed, exuberant arrival; the enormous hedge was established long before we moved into the house.

As with most spring-flowering shrubs, forsythia branches can be cut while the plant is still dormant outside and should open in a vase with the warmth from indoor heat and a good supply of water. The flowers have a long life both on the bush and in a vase. I like to cut them very short and use them as an underpinning in a bowl or vase, as a nice complement to daffodils in the same color shades or as a strong contrast to muscari, hyacinth, and *Fritillaria persica*.

MAGNOLIA

I feel fortunate that there is a star magnolia (*Magnolia stellata*) in front of our house. The small tree has clearly been there for many years, if not decades. I did not realize what it was until I saw photos of its ethereal flowers—of the softest, creamiest white—in Margaret Roach's book *A Way to Garden*. This variety is native to Japan. I like to cut a single branch and leave it alone, simply in a vase, to contemplate. The flower lasts only for a day or so, but others on the branch will continue to open, providing days of blooms.

In the last ten years, I have planted three other magnolias, all of which bloom later than the *stellata*: a *Magnolia* 'Elizabeth', which boasts large, fragrant yellow blossoms; a *Magnolia* 'Venus', whose gorgeous, luminously white flowers I had admired at the home of my friend the garden writer Page Dickey; and a classic pink-and-white magnolia (I wish I knew the exact name) that blooms for weeks. I like to keep a vase filled with the branches of all three in my studio, so that I can enjoy their elegant petals up close while I work away at the pottery wheel.

REDBUD

For many years, I noticed the most gorgeous deep pink tree blooms in locations that seemed surprising to me—along busy roads and in empty lots where it didn't seem that anyone was maintaining them. The flowering branches were a mystery each spring. Once I learned that the tree in question was the native eastern redbud tree (*Cercis canadensis*), I was determined to grow one. I have since planted two. Being a native tree, it isn't fussy about soil or maintenance and, once established, provides years of bloom. (While I waited for my own trees to mature, I would stealthily cut branches from a tree in an empty lot by the side of the road near my house.) The vivid pink color is incomparable, and the cut branches last at least two weeks in a vase.

BLOSSOMING FRUIT TREES

About a decade ago, I started planting a fruit orchard. It took me a while to figure out the right combination and schedule of organic sprays, pruning, and watering. The peach, nectarine, persimmon, quince, apple, apricot, plum, and Asian pear trees now reliably produce good fruit. It is always fraught around the time that they flower, in April and May, as a strong frost will nip the fruit literally in the bud. If the trees make it through this stage, then they must be protected from squirrels climbing up and eating the fruit or birds attacking from above. We try to put metal baffles, or cones, around the trunks to deter the squirrels and will net the trees if we can. All in all, maintaining an orchard is a challenge for the home gardener.

As much as I would like to cut the branches of my trees when they are in flower, that would take away a potential harvest, so I go to a wholesale nursery or specialty market to buy fruit-tree branches instead. It's best to choose unopened branches, which will open in water and provide weeks of bloom indoors. If the branches are left at a nice long length, they can create a great billowing statement in any room. When my fruit trees are pruned in January, I save the cut branches to use as supports in a vase for favorite spring flowers such as hyacinths, daffodils, and tulips.

When I made this simple arrangement, the *Magnolia denudata* (yulan/lily magnolia) branches, which were given to me by Cathy Deutsch of Wave Hill, were in the perfect state of bloom along with the first petite daffodils from my garden. I combined the two in a wood-fired, oribe-glazed footed bowl and added a few pussy willow branches for good measure.

Muscaris

Muscaris boast the most exquisite blues, in shades ranging from the lightest gray-blue to deepest blue-black. They are commonly known as grape hyacinth because their small, urn-shaped flowers cluster like a bunch of grapes, but they are, in fact, part of the lily family (Liliaceae), whereas the common hyacinth is larger and part of the asparagus family (Asparagaceae). The name *muscari* is Greek for "musk," and their scent can be quite strong, despite their delicate size. The odor is so pervasive, in fact, that deer generally avoid them.

To ensure the best selection of muscaris for my arrangements, I make sure to plant one in each hue. My go-to varieties, in order from palest to darkest, include *Muscari aucheri* 'Blue Magic', *M. botryoides* 'Superstar', *M. latifolium*, and *M. paradoxum*. Though it's hard to choose a favorite, mine might be *M. armeniacum* 'Valerie Finnis', named for the wonderfully eccentric English gardener and photographer who passed away in 2006. She knew everything about plants and personalities in the British horticultural world and published one of my favorite books, *Garden People*. Her namesake muscari has nuances of pale blue, pale gray, and a deeper sky blue, with a heavy concentration of florets on the stem (see an example in the photo opposite, farthest right).

These delightful flowers look perfect gathered alone in a vase or grouped with other early blooms like hellebores, hyacinths, and daffodils. They are perennial, but I put in new bulbs each fall, just in case the old ones are disturbed when I'm planting dahlia tubers and annual seeds. They are relatively fuss-free, and the voles don't seem to eat them.

Like crocuses, muscaris are very easy to force. I usually put them in flowerpots, which I then place on the side of the greenhouse, out of the wind but where they can freeze. Sometimes I put leaves around the top of the pot, to insulate the flowers while they are outside; I take the leaves off before bringing the pots back inside, where they add cheer to the studio during the dark days of February. (For more on forcing, see page 271.)

To appreciate the muscari's gorgeous range of blues and the variation of form in the florets, try arranging them in an ombré pattern; this one goes from a dark purplish black to a nuanced slate-blue shade.

Daffodils

Once the leaves of the daffodils start to peek up, my heart leaps a bit. This is a sign that the first true cutting flowers of the growing season will soon arrive. I especially love the acid-yellow daffodils, which are the earliest to bloom and pair perfectly with the yellow forsythia bushes opening nearby the garden. (*Note:* There is some confusion regarding the name of these trumpet-headed blossoms. *Narcissus* is the botanical name for daffodils, and "daffodil" is the common name for all members that fall under the genus *Narcissus*. The American Daffodil Society recommends using the name daffodil except for in scientific writing.)

The first spring that we lived in our house, daffodils exploded around the property. Since then, I have added new types every year, making sure to include daffodils that bloom as early as possible, midseason varieties that bloom alongside the tulips in early May, and late bloomers that are still in flower when the peonies appear in late May. As with all the flowers I cultivate, when ordering daffodil bulbs, I try to cover the range of shapes (trumpet, small-cupped, large-cupped, double), heights (3 to 16 inches/7.5 to 40.6 cm), and colors (pale white, cream, peach, pale pink, and bright acid yellow). All daffodils provide long life in a vase; see page 47 for some of my favorite varieties.

Bulb suppliers are offering their catalogs earlier and earlier, because customers are eager to make their selections as soon as possible. As I write this (at the beginning of May), I just received a notice that ordering for the next spring season is available, which thrills me to no end. I need to order them immediately, before my favorites (and any tempting new varieties) sell out!

HOW TO GROW DAFFODILS

For spring bloom, plant the bulbs anytime from late September till the ground is too hard to dig (bulb suppliers will usually time their deliveries for your appropriate growing zone). Because daffodils contain the toxic chemical lycorine, deer and other animals will not eat them, so you can rest assured they will be left alone no matter where you place them in your yard.

Once planted, daffodils will remain in the garden for many years. Even if neglected, they should return, as they are pretty maintenance-free. Most garden journals advise allowing the leaves and stems to die back in the garden, but I have found that the daffodils survive without any problem even when I cut them back to allow room for other summer and fall seeds and plants. If the bulbs are in a spot where they are happy, the flowers will multiply each season.

A few varieties of daffodil—*Narcissus* 'Barrett Browning', 'Winter Waltz', and 'Tête-à-Tête'—are paired with the equally vibrant forsythia and winter hazel in a grouping of simple white earthenware bottle vases. Together, they make up the essence of seasonal garden bounty.

My favorite aspect of daffodils is the way the colors contrast
from the cup (or corona) to the petals that surround it. Each
type offers a different, always exquisite combination.

If you're too eager for a burst of color to wait until daffodils bloom outdoors in March, consider purchasing pre-cooled bulbs. These can be kept in pots and will bloom indoors earlier in the season, without the need to force; follow the bulb company's instructions for doing so. Both Van Engelen and Colorblends have a great selection of pre-cooled bulbs.

HOW TO ARRANGE DAFFODILS

When I purchase commercially grown daffodils, they are often quite closed up, and the trick of cutting the stems at the bottom and placing them in hot water to encourage the flowers to open does not always succeed. I've had many a bunch just sit there and refuse to open, which is an exercise in frustration. Therefore, when buying daffs in a store, look for those that have already begun to open, even partially. The advantage of forcing or growing one's own flowers is that they can be cut at just the right moment (in the case of daffodils, when they are just showing signs of opening). And, since the harvest is fresh, their vase life can be delightfully long.

FAVORITE VARIETIES

Early Bloomers

***Narcissus* 'Barrett Browning'** A small-cupped daffodil with bright white petals and a deep orange, bowl-shaped corona (cup)

***N.* 'February Gold'** A quintessential sunny-yellow cyclamineus daffodil in miniature form

***N.* 'Little Gem'** A golden yellow miniature trumpet daffodil that's a good candidate for forcing (see page 271)

***N.* 'Rijnveld's Early Sensation'** A trumpet daffodil that's among the first to appear, often popping up through the snow

***N.* 'Tête-à-Tête'** A charming little heirloom cyclamineus variety in classic yellow tones

Mid-Spring Bloomers

***Narcissus* 'April Queen'** An older large-cupped variety with ivory white petals and a large yellow corona with ruffled orange edges

***N.* 'Ice Follies'** A long-lasting large-cupped daffodil with creamy white petals and a large buttery-yellow corona

***N.* 'King Alfred'** An iconic, extremely popular bright yellow trumpet variety worthy of its regal name

***N.* 'Mount Hood'** The petals of this large trumpet stunner are tinged with yellow as they bloom but mature to pure snowy white

***N.* 'Peeping Tom'** A hardy, bright yellow cyclamineus variety known for its long bloom time

Late Bloomers

***Narcissus* 'Cheerfulness'** An heirloom creamy white double daff with touches of orange

***N.* 'Flower Record'** A large-cupped daffodil with a high-contrast combination of a pure white petal perimeter and a flame-orange trumpet at the center

***N.* 'Yellow Cheerfulness'** Similar to its white counterpart, this double buttery-yellow late bloomer is exuberant and wonderfully fragrant

FLOWERS MAKE THE BEST GIFTS

Among the many wonderful reasons to cultivate a cutting garden is this: It fosters generosity. Over the years, I've experienced great joy in sharing an abundance of blooms with friends, family, and clients. The flowers carry my spirit in the same way that I feel my pottery does when it leaves the studio and is used by others as part of their daily lives. What's more, bringing flowers as a gift creates no burden: A bouquet is an ephemeral gesture that can be appreciated as long as it lasts. The recipient can watch the life cycle of a cut flower, meaning every day is a new gift as the bloom changes.

Since I try to grow rare, unusual, and heirloom flower varieties that are not easily found in shops, it's especially gratifying to give them away. I hope their distinctive qualities—the textures, colors, and sizes of the blooms—inspire creativity when the recipients create their own arrangements.

Most flowers have symbolic associations, which can add an extra layer of meaning to the gift. As I've learned from Shane Connolly's book *Discovering the Meaning of Flowers*, red roses represent true love; lilies connote purity and fertility; and the iris symbolizes faith, valor, hope, and wisdom. It's fun to learn about the history of how these floral allegories were assigned.

If I am bringing flowers to a host for lunch or dinner, I wrap the bunch in brown or newsprint paper and tie it together at the bottom with beeswaxed string. If the flowers must survive a lengthy journey, I usually place them in a bucket with water and wrap the bunch when I arrive. When transporting dahlias, I sometimes line the trunk of the car with newsprint and gently lay the stems down flat one by one next to each other so that the heads don't get jostled and break off, which they are apt to do when crowded in a bucket. This is especially important toward the end of the harvest, in autumn, when the stems tend to be weaker than those of the earlier, heavily petaled, dinner-plate types.

Finally, it's good to get in the habit of saving flowers for yourself, too. Rather than waiting for someone to present you with a bouquet, do it for your own enjoyment, as a treat to yourself. I try to remind myself often that just one flower in a bud vase—at the window above the kitchen sink, on the dining table, in the powder room, or by my bed—brings enormous pleasure and a sense of calm.

Seeking Novels
That Are Gay
And Happy

Hyacinths

For years, before I had a garden of my own, I bought cut hyacinths at the flower market in New York City. I love their strong fragrance and their abundance when massed together. Since I started growing them at home in Connecticut, I've found that planting my own (in a garden or forced in a pot, for winter flowering) offers a much wider opportunity for unusual colors and heirloom varieties than when relying solely on commercially grown hyacinths. I also prefer the irregularity of the racemes (small florets) on the homegrown stems.

Before it's time to plant bulbs in fall (usually October here in Connecticut), I purchase a few heirloom hyacinth varieties from Old House Gardens—such as 'City of Haarlem', an exquisite pale yellow color, and 'Roman Blue', a specialty hyacinth imported from the Hortus Bulborum, a legendary Dutch bulb emporium with an incredible collection of hyacinths and tulips. I hope to visit their garden one day in springtime to see their magnificent display.

Hyacinth bulbs can be planted anywhere in the garden or yard, as long as there's adequate sun; their strong smell and poisonous sap keep animals away. The bulbs aren't fussy about soil, requiring just good, organic dirt. They are perennial, but return less flamboyantly each season. I make sure to plant fresh bulbs every year to enjoy their long flowering time in a garden bed.

Hyacinths keep very nicely in the vase, too. I leave them until their last gasp, when the fragrance is too pungent to keep them, though I take care to change the water frequently. In the studio, as I compose photos with these cool, cool blues of early spring, I think of the Danish painter Vilhelm Hammershøi (see page 52). Hammershøi painted his interiors using a monochromatic palette of grays and soft blues, reflecting the northern light of his country. I try to take my photos just as the sun is coming up, as the early light in the studio has a similar cold, Nordic tone in early spring. Sometimes I'll add muscari and a volunteer scilla or two, which randomly appear in the garden at the same time; a few of these contribute nicely to the range of blues in the vase.

When the hyacinths (including *Hyacinthus orientalis* 'Gipsy Queen', 'Delft Blue', 'Pink Pearl', and 'Royal Navy' varieties) have reached their crescendo in the raised beds, it's time to show them off. For display in a widemouthed vase like this one, I cut the stems short, as their heavy heads can cause them to bend from the weight.

Interior Strandgade 30,
Vilhelm Hammershøi,
1900.

FAVORITE VARIETIES

Hyacinthus orientalis **'Anna Liza'** A lavender-pink variety that combines well with hyacinth varieties of all colors

H. orientalis **'City of Haarlem'** A pale ivory-yellow in color that looks amazing as it ages in a vase; returns in the garden reliably each spring

H. orientalis **'Delft Blue'** A pale lilac-blue variety that ages beautifully and is perfect for forcing (see page 271)

H. orientalis **'Fondant'** A bright pink hyacinth that I like to combine with 'Gipsy Queen'

H. orientalis **'Gipsy Queen'** Apricot-salmon color blossoms with highlights of pink and a fragrance that's not too sweet

H. orientalis **'Minos'** A variation of the classic blue hyacinth, with a deeper lilac color that falls between 'Delft Blue' and 'Royal Navy'

H. orientalis **'Royal Navy'** A much darker hyacinth than most, with white outlines; pairs well in a vase with 'Delft Blue'

When I took this photograph of blue and pink hyacinths in a pair of vases one spring morning at dawn, the light mimicked the gray colors of Hammershøi's painting.

Auriculas

To discover auricula primroses is to be captivated by them. With small, varied faces on thick, short stems, they are quite unlike any other flowers. These plants were originally found in the rock fissures of the Alps and are part of the genus *Primula*. Auriculas were first recorded in England in the Elizabethan period, but it wasn't until the eighteenth and nineteenth centuries that enthusiasm for collecting rare specimens rivaled that of the seventeenth-century tulip bulb craze. In the centuries since, the auricula has been hybridized into many enchanting colors; today we can purchase striped and double-form varieties. Like most flowers with obsessive followings, this singular plant boasts societies and exhibitions wholly dedicated to it.

My fascination with these flowers began about fifteen years ago, when my daughter and I saw an exhibit at the Yale Center for British Art in New Haven, Connecticut, on the work of Mrs. Mary Delany, an eighteenth-century British artist who crafted nearly one thousand exquisite paper collages (which she called "mosaics") by hand. We were amazed at how perfectly she captured the essence and construction of each flower.

Her paper auriculas beguiled me, as I was only familiar with this flower in terms of the "theater" that I had studied every spring in the New York Botanical Garden, a tradition inspired by the British, who have produced similar annual displays since the 1800s. An

Primula auricula var., from an album (vol. VII, 99), Mary Delany, 1778.

In an homage to Mary Delany, I set 'Rosemary' and 'Lincoln Chestnut' auricula against a black background. The moodiness of the velvety green leaves contrasts beautifully with the vibrant flowers.

auricula theater resembles a bookcase filled with auriculas in terra-cotta pots and is specially designed to display the plants outdoors, in full bloom. The reason for constructing this growing environment is twofold: The shade mimics the alpine location in which the plants thrive, and the individual pots with the sandy soil keep the flowers cool and sparingly watered.

As my obsession grew, I became determined to learn to grow the plants and build my own theater. I found a wonderful auricula resource in Washington State at Sequim Rare Plants. Once the plants arrived, I mixed potting soil with sand for improved drainage, then placed each seedling in the mixture within its own small terra-cotta pot. In recent years, I have been keeping the plants in the greenhouse over the winter, where they seem to flourish, producing plenty of flowers for display.

A few years ago, when I was visiting the Sissinghurst Castle Garden in England, I saw the most beautiful wooden hutch filled with blooming bulbs in terra-cotta pots on the outer wall of Vita Sackville-West's bedroom and library. I thought it was the perfect design for an auricula theater. I roughly estimated the dimensions and took a photograph that I later showed to my friend Larry Liggett, an exceptionally talented woodworker. We collaborated to re-create the piece, which I now use to hold my auriculas. It was exactly what I longed for.

Sacheverell Sitwell wrote in his 1939 book *Old Fashioned Flowers*, "The first moment of seeing a Stage Auricula [theater] is an experience never to be forgotten." I am thrilled to have one of my own in which to display the dainty flowers each spring.

FAVORITE VARIETIES

Primula auricula **'Black Star'** Single rows of dark red petals with white centers

P. auricula **'Brownie'** Deep burnt-orange double flowers that are ruffled like a cancan dancer's skirt; provides a nice contrast to auriculas with simpler, single rows of petals

P. auricula **'Cornmeal'** Dusty green outer petals with black-and-white centers

P. auricula **'Green Shank'** An arresting variety edged with pale green and with red, white, and yellow toward the center

P. auricula **'Old Mustard'** Most intriguing mustard yellow petals with white centers

PART II

VERNAL

I AM A TRUE BELIEVER IN THE ADAGE THAT HOPE springs eternal. From roughly early May through the middle of June, that trust is reinforced by a flurry of activity out my window. The vernal season is filled with reassurance; it's a reminder of seasons past and of the constancy of nature, despite all odds. Bleeding hearts feel especially appropriate as a marker of this deeply expressive period of garden growth.

This is the time for starting the seeds I wish to direct-sow and unboxing the dahlia tubers after their long winter slumber in the basement. I liken the process to greeting old friends and am excited to put the tubers in the ground again to see them bloom a few months hence. The flower plugs are also planted in the garden beds, positioned to fit around the perennials that have begun to protrude from the soil.

Things are ramping up outside, the days are longer, and soon I am back to plotting out how on earth I will capture my favorite specimens of spring before it's too late. I do my best and persist with the cutting and arranging, all the while remaining optimistic that whatever happens, there will be another chance next year to try my hand at filling the garden with more seasonal beauty.

Lilacs

The scent of lilacs instantly reminds me of my grandmother. She so loved the flowers that she sprinkled lilac water on her clothes, regardless of the season. She often took the bus from New York City to visit us in New Jersey, where we had several lilac bushes planted around our yard. On her birthday, May 9, we would place a vase of lilacs by her bed; my birthday is just four days later, so we shared a great kinship about this time of year and the flowers that mark it.

Though lilacs come in a range of colors, the name originates from the Arabic word *laylak* and the Persian word *nylac*, both meaning "blue." The flowers are native to the Balkan region of Europe but were highly cultivated in France.

Like the redbud tree (see page 40), lilac bushes seem to thrive on neglect. The most stupendous displays are quite often seen by the road or a house whose owners clearly haven't touched them in years. I have a couple of white lilac bushes that bloom wonderfully each May, along with others of all varieties—from the darkest purple and variegated purples to the palest lavender—that continue to thrive. I have read that spent blooms on the bush should be chopped off to promote next year's flowers, but again, I know that no one is pruning those highway lilacs yet they seem perfectly happy. I tend to follow suit, leaving the lilac bushes alone and hoping for the best for next year's harvest.

Cut lilacs don't always last long in a vase. Once placed in water, the display must be enjoyed immediately, as the branches might begin to wilt shortly after cutting. There are strategies one can employ to keep the cut flowers sprightly, such as slicing open the stem from the bottom and splitting the branch up a couple of inches (5 cm), which allows the water in the vase to hydrate them longer. To be honest, I find this method to be a crapshoot. I do strip the leaves up to the blossoms upon cutting the stem off the bush, which helps. For the short while they last, lilacs pair perfectly with peonies, bearded irises, and dogwood branches. I love the exuberant explosion of color, perfume, and shape that combines all of these seasonal beauties.

Lilacs such as 'Sensation', 'President Lincoln', and the common white *alba* variety are combined here with the white lily tulip and an early-blooming heirloom *Iris germanica*. The crisp whites add a great freshness to the bouquet.

FAVORITE VARIETIES

Syringa vulgaris 'Aucubaefolia' Fragrant double flowers of lavender blue, with variegated heart-shaped leaves

S. vulgaris 'Primrose' Creamy yellow-white, sweetly fragrant flowers

S. vulgaris 'Sensation' Large rich purple florets edged in white

S. × hyacinthiflora 'Pocahontas' Lovely fragrance with deep blue-purple flowers

FLOWER-TOPPED SUGAR COOKIES

I loved to bake and decorate cookies with my children when they were young and still at home. Though all three now live far away, in different parts of the world, I often send them treats by mail. When these sugar cookies arrive, I imagine that my garden has traveled to meet them.

Throughout the growing season, many colorful and edible garden flowers are perfect for adorning cookies (and cakes). I use a combination of lilac, violet, auricula, primrose, nasturtium, dogtooth lily, geranium, lily, and tulip. You may choose pesticide-free edible flower varieties that you grow yourself or purchase organically grown blossoms. *Makes about 2 dozen*

4 cups (480 g) sifted all-purpose flour,
   plus more for dusting
1 teaspoon baking powder
½ teaspoon salt
½ pound (2 sticks/225 g) unsalted butter, at
   room temperature
2 cups (395 g) sugar, plus more for sprinkling

2 large eggs
Finely grated zest of 2 lemons
2 teaspoons fresh lemon juice
1 teaspoon vanilla extract
A few handfuls fresh organically grown
   edible flower blossoms or petals

In a large bowl, whisk together the flour, baking powder, and salt.

With an electric mixer, beat the butter and sugar on medium-high speed until pale and fluffy, 3 to 5 minutes. Add the eggs one at a time, scraping down the sides of the bowl as needed. With the mixer on low speed, add the flour mixture and beat just until combined. Mix in the lemon zest, lemon juice, and vanilla.

Transfer the dough to a large piece of plastic wrap, seal, and chill until firm, at least 30 minutes or up to 3 days.

Preheat the oven to 325°F (165°C). Line two large baking sheets with parchment.

Divide the dough into quarters. Working with one quarter at a time, dust the dough lightly with flour and place between two sheets of parchment. Roll out the dough to ⅛-inch (3 mm) thickness.

Using a 3-inch (7.5 cm) cookie cutter, cut the dough into rounds and transfer to a prepared baking sheet, spacing them 2 inches (5 cm) apart. Repeat with the remaining dough. Place a few flowers or petals onto each round, gently pressing them into the tops. Sprinkle the tops evenly with sugar.

Bake until the edges start to brown, 8 to 10 minutes. Transfer the cookies to wire racks to cool.

Tulips

I am continually inspired by classic Dutch still life paintings of tulips, particularly Margareta Haverman's 1716 *A Vase of Flowers*, on view at the Metropolitan Museum of Art in New York City. The tulip in this canvas is placed in a center line of white and pink flowers, with its variegated white-and-red petals culminating at the top middle. Although my aim is never to try to replicate exactly what I see in an image, I often reference paintings such as Haverman's, as well as photographs that feature exquisite colors and forms, when deciding which tulip bulbs to plant.

A Vase of Flowers,
Margareta Haverman, 1716.

The rare tulips shown in my favorite Dutch still life paintings are still cultivated at the Hortus Bulborum in the Netherlands, which specializes in preserving antique tulips. Old House Gardens in Michigan, a wonderful source of heirloom bulbs, occasionally offers tulips from the Hortus, although they are quite expensive. Since I continually worry about the voles having their way with the tulips, I order bulbs from other purveyors that aren't quite so dear (see page 67 for a few of my favorites).

Tulips are characterized by shape and bloom times, and there are some fifteen different categories; I try to choose from as many of these as possible each fall, with an eye toward how each will lend its distinctive profile and character to voluminous seasonal arrangements. Examples include the fringed, parrot, peony, and lily varieties (the latter two are not to be confused with their namesake flower species). The first tulips to appear in spring are the species tulip, which are smaller and naturalize more freely than commercially hybridized (specifically cross-bred) tulips. They are wild tulips that originated in the mountains of Europe and eastern Asia. I love their delicate stems and petals as

A sampling of tulip varieties from a recent growing season demonstrates how any color or shape of petal can be grouped together.

well as their gorgeous colors. They are perfectly in scale with the early daffodils, hyacinths, and muscaris that join them in the spring garden. Their delicate heads open brilliantly in the sun each day and close at night—both in the garden and in a vase. Midseason tulips bloom at the same time as daffodils, hyacinths, and fritillaries. The late tulips appear almost at the end, when the lilacs, peonies, and roses begin to bloom.

HOW TO GROW TULIPS

Species tulips are perennial, as are other tulips that fall under the classification "botanical tulips." Though many of my tulips return (unless they were eaten by the squirrels or voles in summer), I can't resist ordering new bulbs each late spring or summer, to arrive just as fall flowers are waning.

Planting tulips is a straightforward process. I put the bulbs in trenches in the garden after I have dug up the dahlia tubers, usually in mid to late November (before the ground freezes, although I have sometimes planted as late as January with no problem). The tulips can just as easily be planted in pots, alone or layered with daffodils and hyacinth bulbs; let them sit outside over the winter and they will reward you with an explosion of color and scent come spring.

Tulips blooming in the round garden. The bulbs are planted closely together in long trenches in autumn, in no particular order. I tend to mix different types and look forward to the surprise of color when they open in spring.

FAVORITE VARIETIES

Tulipa clusiana '**Lady Jane**' A bright red-and-white species with petals that open fully in the sun

T. praestans '**Shogun**' A multiheaded bright orange species that returns reliably

T. sylvestris A petite species tulip in the most marvelous yellow, perfect in bud vases alone or with tiny daffodils

T. '**Blushing Lady**' A pale yellow-and-pink giant Darwin tulip with an enormous head and a 30-inch (76 cm) stem (a favorite in tulipieres and tall vases)

T. '**Carnaval de Nice**' A classic old-world red-and-white peony tulip that blooms around my birthday (May 13)

T. '**Dream Touch**' A double tulip with magenta-plum petals edged with white

T. '**Flaming Parrot**' A huge tulip with yellow-and-red frilled petals that are a sight for sore eyes after the long winter

T. '**Gavota**' A deep maroon-and-yellow triumph tulip, which is a cross between a Darwin and an early-blooming tulip

T. '**Miranda**' A scarlet-red double tulip that blooms late and is especially brilliant in a vase

T. '**Monsella**' A cheery bright yellow double tulip with red streaks on the petals

T. '**Orange Emperor**' A great option for displaying in a tulipiere, thanks to its tall stems and large, bold orange flower heads

T. '**Palmyra**' I love the drama of this dark black-burgundy, perfectly egg-shaped double tulip with ivory interiors

T. '**Paul Scherer**' A great black-purple single midseason tulip

HOW TO ARRANGE TULIPS

Tulips can be cut when they are still closed. Some growers pull out the entire plant, bulb and all. Depending on what I'm looking for, I cut them at various stages of bloom. They are wonderful to mass in quantity in a vase, either a single type or a combination of types that are blooming simultaneously. Or I mix them with other bulbs and flowering branches, such as viburnum and forsythia.

Two other works of art come to mind when I begin to arrange my tulips. The

first is a wonderfully surreal photograph by André Kertész titled *Melancholic Tulip*, from 1939. The artist used a parabolic mirror that he had brought from Paris to New York. Tulips would have just arrived in the flower market from Holland in February, indeed the darkest time of winter. I love how Kertész has distorted the vase and stem to create a self-portrait that captures his state of mind at the time. The tulip is portrayed as a two-dimensional object rather than a more recognizable flower. I, too, like to look

My tulipieres are inspired by seventeenth-century Delft spouted vases and designed to support the stems of freshly cut tulips during the height of their season. This white earthenware pair has a sense of humor and allows the riot of tulip colors and shapes to explode from the spouts.

at flowers abstractly, and find the tulip to be the perfect model for doing so. The petals and stem, as separate parts, are incredibly expressive, depending on the variety and color. Emperor, single early, triumph, and single late tulips are among my favorite types, for their strong forms as well as the vibrant color options; all last wonderfully long once cut and displayed.

Those qualities led me to the second photograph that I study. In 1994, the American photographer Lee Friedlander was laid up at home with sore knees. This sedentary period was most unusual, since he is known for traveling the country to photograph his subjects. Friedlander started examining flowers that his wife had placed around the rooms and became intrigued with the tulip stems as forms by themselves. Later he produced a wonderful book with the photographic series that resulted from this unplanned home study. I love the idea of focusing on just the beauty of the stem and disregarding the actual bloom. It implies that there is beauty in all parts and small details should not be overlooked.

Melancholic Tulip, André Kertész, 1939.

New City, New York, Lee Friedlander, 1994.

Polypodium Phegopteris,
Anna Atkins, 1853.

PHOTOGRAPHY AND FLOWERS
GO HAND IN HAND

The long and storied relationship between flowers and photography continually captivates me. From the moment of photography's inception, people have striven to capture the essence of flowers at the height of their beauty, and this is what I try to honor as I take portraits of my pottery filled with flowers from my garden. There are infinite ways to creatively use the camera, and I will never cease seeking out new ways to approach the process.

I continually study the work of some of the earliest photographers, all the way back to the daguerreotype. One particular favorite daguerreotype by "Cromer's Amateur" (the photographer is unknown) circa 1845 is titled *Bouquet of Flowers* and features an Instagram-worthy vase of dahlias and other blooms.

One of my garden photography idols is John Frederick William Herschel. You could call him an original multihyphenate, as his bio includes mathematician, inventor, astronomer, chemist, and botanist among his careers. In 1839, Herschel devised a sensitized paper to capture images and then the fixing formula to keep them from fading off the paper. He coined the term *photography* (derived from Greek words meaning "light" and "writing") and expanded the definitions of *emulsion*, *positive*, and *negative* to apply to this new art form. He also invented the anthotype and cyanotype.

Bouquet of Flowers,
"Cromer's Amateur"
(unknown), ca. 1845.

In 1842, Herschel taught the cyanotype technique to John George Children, a chemist and zoologist, who then passed that knowledge along to his daughter Anna Atkins, a botanist and photographer. In 2018, I saw the most exquisite exhibition of Atkins's work at the New York Public Library, which featured cyanotype prints in a darkened room in beautifully designed cases. Atkins produced the first photographic illustrated book, *Photographs of British Algae: Cyanotype Impressions*, in 1843. She made a solution of iron salts that she used to coat paper, and then placed botanical specimens on top and exposed the plates in the sun. The result was a collection of intriguing silhouettes of plants against a gorgeous blue background. Since seeing the exhibit, I've been experimenting with cyanotypes using natural specimens from my garden and have specifically landed on the anthotype process because it is nontoxic and works with flowers, leaves, and vegetables. The technique is easy and great fun. (See page 75 for a tutorial.)

The photography of Charles Jones has also greatly inspired the way I think about still life composition. What I relate to most is how Jones lovingly grew fruits, vegetables, and flowers from seed to harvest and knew them intimately. No one else could have captured the images as he did, which informs the way I approach my own garden, as well as my photography efforts in the studio. He produced an extraordinary group of images at the turn of the twentieth century while working at Great Ote Hall near Burgess Hill, in Sussex, England. Not much is known about Jones's life. His photos were forgotten until hundreds of prints were discovered in a trunk twenty-two years after his death. He obviously took great pride in the flowers and vegetables that he grew and photographed in a simple and elegant fashion. Sadly, none of the negatives from his glass plate camera have survived. A couple of years ago, I saw a rare collection of his photographs and bought the catalog so I could reference them often. The gold-toned gelatin silver prints have incredible detail and character.

Another of my heroes of the photographic world is Edward Steichen, who learned each new technical photographic advancement as it came along. He was one of the first American photographers to learn color photography from the French Lumière brothers in the early twentieth century. He also made haunting photogravures and gelatin silver prints. In 1902, he cofounded the Photo-Secession group with Alfred Stieglitz in New York City, which organized photo exhibitions, and he designed a photo art journal titled *Camera Work*. He combined art photography and commercial photography as head photographer for Condé Nast and then went on to be the director of photography at the Museum of Modern Art, organizing more than fifty shows, including the groundbreaking *Family of Man* exhibition in 1955. He was also an avid gardener (particularly of delphiniums). His entire biography fascinates me greatly.

Although I use a digital camera in my work, it is my goal to continually study historical techniques, as I think the results add such nuance to the pictures, especially in the realm of flower still lifes.

Iris, Charles Jones, ca. 1900.

Delphiniums,
Edward Steichen,
1940.

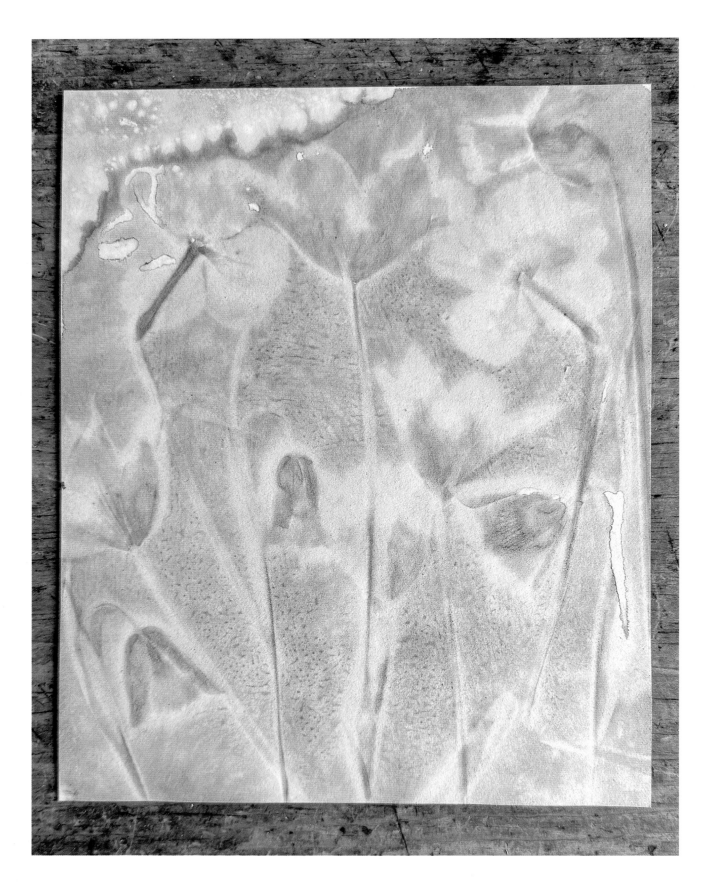

MAKING FLOWER ANTHOTYPES

I have long been interested in the history of photography and early photographic discoveries. An anthotype, from the Greek *anthos*, for "flower," and *typos*, for "imprint," is a photograph made by means of light-sensitive juices extracted from plants and flowers that have been brushed on paper. An object or transparency with a positive image is placed on the treated paper and exposed under the sun (or, in its place, an ultraviolet lamp). Ultimately a photographic image results.

John Herschel is usually credited as the inventor of the anthotype (though Mary Somerville is often cited as one of the researchers of the process), and he experimented broadly with its possibilities. The process is low-tech, nontoxic (as long as you avoid using poisonous plants), and lots of fun. (It is a perfect project to do with children.) The results are quite beautiful, and there are no chemicals or messy darkroom procedures to deal with.

The image appears very, very slowly, so patience is required, especially in seasons or on days when the sun is not strong. You'll get the best results during the long, sunny days of summer through early fall, but you can always use a UV lamp to try the process indoors or at a darker time of year.

I find the most exciting part of the whole process comes in experimenting with the materials for the emulsion. For my anthotype emulsion, I used geranium flowers from the plants in my greenhouse. For the second part, choosing materials for the image, I placed a selection of spring blooms directly onto the emulsion-coated paper.

An anthotype I made in April from freshly picked tulips, daffodils, and fritillaries.

Tools & Materials

Plant material

Mortar and pestle (*not* one used in the kitchen)

1 to 2 tablespoons grain alcohol (I use Everclear)

1 (12-inch/30 cm) square double layer of cheesecloth

Low wide bowl, for the emulsion

Flexible spatula (3-inch/7.5 cm size is ideal)

Rubber gloves

Scissors

2 (8-by-10-inch/20 by 25 cm) sheets 100% cotton paper (I use Hahnemühle Platinum Rag)

1 (3-inch-wide/7.5 cm) foam brush

1 (3-inch-wide/7.5 cm) Japanese hake brush

1 cardboard-backed glass frame (an 11-by-14-inch/ 28 by 36 cm clip frame works well)

8 (1-inch/2.5 cm) binder clips

UV lamp (optional in the sunny season)

Prepare the emulsion: Gather enough flowers (anything you've harvested from your own garden or purchased or foraged responsibly) to fill the mortar two times. Crush the flower petals in the mortar and pestle. Mix 1 tablespoon of the alcohol with the petals in the mortar. Add up to another tablespoon alcohol, if needed, but don't add too much—you don't want the emulsion to be watery. (I had more petals than would fit comfortably into the mortar basin, so I crushed them in two batches, using 1 tablespoon of alcohol in each batch.)

Drape the cheesecloth over the bowl, then use the spatula to transfer the mixture from the mortar onto the cheesecloth (take care to collect all of the liquid).

Wearing rubber gloves, pull up the sides of the cheesecloth, making a ball of crushed petals and holding all the ends in one hand. With the other hand, repeatedly squeeze the juice into the bowl until you feel that you have extracted as much liquid as possible from the cheesecloth. Discard the cheesecloth and compost the plant matter.

Prepare the paper: Ideally move into a darkened room for this step, to limit sun exposure on the paper. Cut sheets of the cotton paper to your desired size (or leave whole) and place them next to the bowl of emulsion. Dip the foam brush into the emulsion and brush it onto the paper, going up and down to start and then back and forth horizontally to ensure an even coat. Smooth the surface of the emulsion using the hake brush.

Let the paper dry in the darkened room and then brush with another coat of emulsion. It is better to build up the density of the color gradually than to try to work on it while wet. The strength of the final image's color will depend upon the plant material used for the emulsion and how many coats you apply. For my geranium emulsion, I brushed five coats onto the paper over the period of a day, letting the paper dry completely between each coat.

Lay out the image: Once the paper is completely dry, place it on the cardboard back of a clip frame and arrange flowers on top of the paper as you wish. Carefully place the glass on top of the flowers so as not to move them too much, then use the binder clips to hold the glass in place. Make sure that the clips do not cover the emulsion-coated paper, or they will leave a mark.

Expose the image: Place the frame holding the paper directly in the sun, or under a UV lamp, making sure there aren't any obstructions. (Put any unused treated sheets into a cardboard box, out of the light, to prevent them from fading.)

The exposure time will depend on many variables, including whether you use the sun or the lamp. The paper, emulsion, and objects placed on the paper will also influence exposure time. It can be as short as 30 minutes, though it can easily take much longer. Anthotypes are a slow process. Periodically check the setup by removing the glass and carefully lifting the plant matter to see if you are satisfied with the image produced. Remember to be patient! Once you're happy with the image, remove the glass and plant matter. If fresh plant materials were used, they can be composted.

Keep in mind that the nature of anthotype is ephemeral, which contributes to its distinct beauty and meaning. Over time, exposure to light can cause the color and the image to fade, so take care to keep your finished piece away from direct sunlight.

I placed the geranium-treated paper and flowers outside in the sun in the morning and brought them inside at night for weeks. The deep fuchsia color of the paper softened to a soft taupe, and the flowers produced silhouettes in the most beautiful shade of lilac.

Peonies

I have known peonies all my life, since my mother grew the bushes in our New Jersey garden. These herbaceous perennials are not only the most romantic flowers, in my opinion, but they also grow increasingly beautiful as they age. Whenever I see one in bloom, I think of Degas's ballet dancers' tutus and Édouard Manet's painting *Peonies*, which is at the Metropolitan Museum in New York City.

When Wally and I moved to our current house, I was thrilled to discover old peony bushes still growing strong. Since then, I have collected and added peony plants wherever I manage to find space. Some are gifts from friends' gardens, and others were purchased from local plant nurseries and peony specialists I found online.

A farm near our house grew the most wonderful peonies for many years. The farmer, who lived to age 102, sold them in bunches of five blossoms at his small stand by the road. One of his tricks was to wait until a bit of color showed above the bud covers (called sepals) before he cut them to ensure that the bud would open. I asked him every growing season if I might have one of his peony plants for my garden, as I loved the provenance, but he always refused. To this day, I wish I could have convinced him to share.

The range of shapes, colors, petal sizes, configurations, and bloom times is broad for peonies. The American Peony Society lists six standard forms: single, Japanese, anemone, semidouble, bomb, and full double. I have chosen several versions of these forms, in colors ranging from white to the deepest red. Toward the end of May, I can see the first flowers of the Japanese woodland, tree, and single herbaceous peonies coming into bloom. The rest emerge throughout the month of June.

Peonies were named after Pæon, the physician to the gods in Greek mythology, and are believed to have healing properties; legend has it that he used the root to treat Zeus for an injury. In their native China, peonies' dried roots have been used for medicinal purposes for centuries (they are recorded as far back as 10,000 BCE). From China, the peony made its way to Japan, where the flower remains highly prized.

HOW TO GROW PEONIES

It takes several seasons for a peony plant to establish itself, but by adhering to a few gardening techniques, you can ensure that it grows and produces more flowers every year. With proper care, a peony plant can last for decades. (Thankfully, the flowers do not appeal to deer.)

Peonies like full sun and are not fussy about the soil but should not be planted too deep in the ground. I find that each bush blooms stronger if the stems are

Lush, coral-colored tree peonies are supported by viburnum branches in this footed terra-cotta bowl and combined with roses and bearded iris.

held upright with metal peony supports. I apply an organic fertilizer in early spring and fall.

If you, like me, have made the mistake of placing peony plants in the wrong spot, where it was too shady or there wasn't enough space for them to grow, know that it's not difficult to transplant them in autumn. The clumps are also easy to split into two or more plants to increase your bounty.

Over the course of the season and well after blooming, peony stalks and leaves turn brown. If I have time, I cut the brown parts away. The sprouts for next year are already at the base of the plant, so trimming needs to be done carefully so that next year's blooms aren't damaged. I put a light layer of fallen leaves over the plant to protect it over the winter. If I am very busy and don't have a chance to do this pruning, I wait until early spring to trim the old stalks. As I write this in late March, I am able to cut back the stalks from last spring's flowers and can already see this year's growth pushing out of the ground.

HOW TO ARRANGE PEONIES

These luxurious flowers bloom at a joyful time of the year, coinciding with the late tulips, early roses, lilacs, bearded irises, bleeding hearts, and dogwoods, to name just a few. In fact, there is so much bursting into flower with the arrival of warm weather—finally—in the Northeast, I always have an abundance of

FAVORITE VARIETIES

Paeonia lactiflora **'Festiva Maxima'** An especially popular variety thanks to its voluminous pure-white flower heads with flecks of crimson

P. lactiflora **'Georgiana Shaylor'** A large, frilly, light rose–pink peony that graces the garden in late midseason

P. **'Bartzella'** A large, lush yellow intersectional (cross between tree and herbaceous) variety with a long bloom window

P. **'Buckeye Belle'** A semidouble flower with velvety, beautifully deep red blooms

P. **'Coral Charm'** An early-blooming beauty with dark green leaves and petals that change from deep coral-pink to peach to white over time

P. **'Duchess de Nemours'** A wonderfully fragrant variety with creamy white double petals

P. **'Kopper Kettle'** Named for its mix of red, yellow, and orange petals that produce a stunning coppery effect

plant material to work with. Tree peonies, such as 'Sonoma Sisters' or 'Cao Zhou Hong', are especially dramatic in a small group or simply one stem in a vase. The nuanced color of the petals is different from those of the herbaceous peony types.

It's a luxury to grow your own peonies, but they are one of the best flower varieties to buy as cut stems; each stage is perfect for display, even as they decline. Where I live, there is usually a good supply of locally grown peonies in season. I give the stems a fresh cut and strip the leaves before putting them into a vase. Tightly closed buds will unfurl over time when the stems are placed in warm water. I leave them in a vase until the last petals fall from the centers.

An armload of herbaceous peonies from my garden ready for arranging include 'Lady Alexandra Duff', 'Coral Charm', 'Doctor Alexander Fleming', and 'Coral Sunset', among other beauties.

Azaleas

I have thought about azaleas since I was sixteen years old, when I first read about them in the novel *Rebecca* by Daphne du Maurier. While walking in the garden, the unnamed narrator puts her hand in the pocket of a raincoat that belonged to her husband's first wife, the late Rebecca, and pulls out a handkerchief that carried with it a faint scent of azalea. I loved the sense of romance and mystery lingering in a long-forgotten piece of cloth. Since then, I have considered scent an important characteristic for flowers.

Azaleas are native to China and Japan. In 2013, when I took part in a residency program in porcelain in Jingdezhen, China, our group took a trip to the mountains, where azaleas and rhododendrons bloomed on the mountainside. We were told that the flowers had been cultivated by Chinese monks.

When Wally and I moved into our current house in Weston, there was a magnificent scarlet-red azalea bush and a few smaller ones in a salmon-pink tone on the property. I don't know the names of these varieties; however, azaleas are easily found at plant nurseries in springtime. The first couple of winters that we lived in this house, deer ate the bushes, which greatly compromised the bloom. We should've sprayed the azaleas with an organic deer repellent in fall to protect them over the colder months.

Since we began doing that, they have performed beautifully. Having the bushes professionally pruned has also added to the health of these plants.

It takes a few seasons for azaleas to establish themselves, but thereafter, they bloom reliably. Where I live, this happens around Mother's Day, at the same time that the bearded irises begin to appear. Both flowers work well together in arrangements, along with tulips, lilacs, and late-blooming daffodils. I like to use the blooming branches as the support system in a vase or bowl. They provide a firm base for the flowers, helping to anchor them in place; the branches also add a welcome bit of wildness.

Opposite: A porcelain bowl glazed in tenmoku and kaki holds deep pink azaleas and bleeding hearts (with the help of a flower frog).

Below: The azalea bushes on our property hug the house. I am grateful to see these grandes dames reappear each May.

The incredibly vibrant fuchsia azalea bush inspired an arrangement that includes boldly colored tulips, primulas, and muscaris, all set in a trio of tea dust–glazed vases before a saturated pink backdrop.

Bearded Irises

The name *iris* comes from the Greek word for "rainbow" (which is also the name of the Greek goddess of the rainbow). This is a fitting name for a flower that offers seemingly infinite possibilities for variation and nuance in color. Of all the varieties of iris that exist (around three hundred, by some estimates), the bearded ones are what I grow (and arrange, and photograph) in earnest. The flower heads can be beautifully bitone (two-colored) or magnificently monochromatic, with some gorgeously intricate patterns on the petals of certain varieties, too. Without fail, when the bearded irises appear in the garden each year, I wonder, How do the colors or petal striations happen? They constantly astound me—so much that I struggle to limit the number of new ones I choose to plant.

My fascination with the bearded iris began in earnest in the late 1990s, on a garden tour of Provence. At one grand estate, we saw an enormous bowl just inside the entryway filled with deep blue bearded irises that were replaced every

Bearded irises are gathered in a trio of wood-fired pitchers along with roses and tree peonies. Putting multiple vases together creates the illusion of one large arrangement; in this case, the narrow openings hold the flower stems together nicely, without additional support.

Iris Seedlings, Sir Cedric Morris, 1943.

day. This struck me as the utmost in luxury. Throw those flowers out every day? Can you imagine? Since then, I've learned that one only need pull off the spent iris bloom and the stalk continues to open. But I will always have the vision of the gorgeous room with the bowl filled to the brim with the most beautiful flowers.

In 2018, a magical exhibition of Cedric Morris's iris paintings at the Garden Museum in London gave me a new appreciation of the history of this flower. Morris not only painted bearded iris portraits, he also cultivated the plants and introduced them for sale. Since that

'Edith Wolford'   'Harvest of Memories'   'Victoria Falls'
'Feel the Thunder'   'Before the Storm'   'Pallida Dalmatica'
'Fall Fiesta'   'Wench'   'Benton Cordelia'

'Malheur'
'Dollface'
'Haunted Heart'

'Bee My Honey'
'Cubs Win It'
'Rum Is the Reason'

'Toucan Tango'
'Downtown Brown'
'Best Bet'

exhibit, there has been a great revival of interest in these historic flowers.

Though purchasing Cedric Morris corms in the United States is currently out of reach, there are many exquisite varieties available. The first two that I planted were a pale blue, similar to 'Victoria Falls', shared from my sister-in-law's garden, and an orange iris that I bought at a plant sale at the Battery Conservancy in New York City, in the garden that Piet Oudolf designed. I get a bit bolder in my choices with each growing season, adding more and more varieties as I consider their bloom time, reblooming (early and late), and, of course, color!

Bearded irises are challenging to photograph because the petals have many folds; the interior, which has its own separate coloring, is even more intriguing but hard to capture. I strive to document the nuances of the form.

HOW TO GROW BEARDED IRISES

I seek out heirloom varieties of bearded iris from garden friends and from a number of specialty growers. (See page 280 for a list of my favorite sources.) My advice is to look through a company's catalog and select the colors and forms that appeal to you most. I guarantee you will be back the next fall ordering more.

Bearded irises grow from rhizomes, which are planted shallowly (a couple of inches/6 cm below the surface of the soil) in fall. I have sometimes received my new plants in September and for various reasons have forgotten to put them in the ground until just before frost. Nevertheless, they have done fine in spring, and I appreciate these flowers for their flexibility as well as their aesthetic appeal.

My first bearded iris flowers begin blooming in early May and the last one flowers in mid-June. I recently carved out new flower beds to accommodate the heirloom varieties. Because the iris does not appeal to the deer, I can plant them outside of the fenced-in gardens, which are bursting, and along the old stone walls that surround the house. In fact, they can be placed almost anywhere without too much worry. Bearded irises aren't fussy; if they get full sun, they should multiply in successive growing seasons. I always cut off the spent stems once the flowers have stopped blooming.

To increase the health of the plants and encourage subsequent blooms, it helps to divide bearded irises every three years; otherwise, the number of blooming stems will diminish. This is also a wonderful strategy to increase your iris stock without purchasing more rhizomes.

HOW TO ARRANGE BEARDED IRISES

Bearded irises are not commonly sold as cut flowers in the market, perhaps because they are more fragile than the blue Siberian iris, which is grown commercially and sold closed, so that it will open in a vase. The Siberians have their merits, but to me they lack the beautiful color nuances of the true garden–grown bearded varieties.

Each year, I experiment making differently shaped vases to set off the bearded irises to their best advantage. Tall, narrow shapes are helpful to support the strong stems; otherwise, I place a grouping of irises in a great low bowl that can hold a flower frog, which allows for better observation of the petal and color formation (and the best perspective for photographs, too).

Once cut, bearded irises last exceedingly well in a vase. One must delicately snap off the spent blooms so that the ones below will open. Sometimes a lower stem coming off the main branch can be cut off and placed in a vase on its own. It is also helpful to take off this side stem to make placing the main stem in a tall vase easier. I like to combine bearded irises with peonies, roses, and blooming branches such as viburnum and dogwood.

Arranged in a bowl with a flower frog, azaleas cover the bearded iris stems but allow the blooms to be admired.

FAVORITE VARIETIES

Iris '**Awakening Embers**' Dark purple-red color with an orange inflection

I. '**Before the Storm**' A deep blue-black-purple variety that's also a vigorous grower

I. '**Champagne Elegance**' White standard with delicate taupe-apricot falls and a lovely fragrance

I. '**Downtown Brown**' Taupe, purple, lavender, yellow; colors transform as the flower ages

I. '**Edith Wolford**' A rich buttercup standard and violet-blue falls

I. '**Immortality**' A bright white iris that (amazingly) reblooms in fall

I. '**Insaniac**' White falls with burgundy and yellow stripes

I. '**On Deck**' A creamy yellow standard with blue and violet falls

I. '**Sun Devil**' Yellow top and burgundy falls make this iris all velvet

I. '**Toucan Tango**' Crazy mustard and violet stripes throughout its flower head

Dogwoods and Viburnums

These two shrubs bloom simultaneously, a bit later than the flowering trees of early spring (page 36). Their blossoms are mostly creamy white, except for those of the beautiful pink Japanese dogwood, which I grow and cut for arrangements. Unlike some of the sturdier flowering trees, these two don't last as long in the vase, however.

DOGWOOD

When I was growing up, the dogwood tree in my family's yard in Morristown, New Jersey, was the perfect size for climbing: not so small that I damaged the branches when I ascended, but not so large that I could climb to a dangerous height. I liked to sit in the middle of the tree and sing to myself, or look over into the next yard, like Rapunzel, and stare at our neighbor's rosebushes. (We were not allowed into that garden, but I loved to watch the woman weaving in and out of the rows with her gloves and pruning shears.)

Many years later, I inherited a beautiful dogwood from the previous owners of our current home in Weston. Unfortunately, the tree was damaged when we put in a septic system. I didn't replace that exact variety, but I did find a delicate Japanese dogwood (*Cornus kousa*) that boasted the loveliest pink flowers with olive green centers. I planted it in a sunny spot near two magnolias and surrounded it with fencing a couple of feet (1 m) from the trunk to prevent deer from eating the leaves and flowers. The branches pair nicely in vases with the early peonies and tulips.

Here and opposite: A pink Japanese dogwood blooms reliably in our yard every June. The tones of the flowers in this arrangement (dogwood, roses, peonies, geums, foxgloves, salvias, and bearded irises) complement the pale blue celadon glaze on the porcelain vase.

VIBURNUM

More than thirty years ago, I received a native mapleleaf viburnum (*Viburnum acerifolium*) as a gift from a friend. I placed it near the side of our house, where it has continued to bloom reliably without much trouble every year since. The flowers have a strong scent, and for some reason, our old dog Peter loved to chew on the leaves (we scattered his ashes at the base of the shrub so that he would always be there when it blooms). In autumn, this viburnum has lovely, deep blue-black berries and crimson leaves that work well in seasonal arrangements with dahlias and asters.

I have another type, *Viburnum plicatum* f. *tomentosum*, or doublefile viburnum, with clusters of flowers that slightly resemble a hydrangea. This opens a bit later in early May and works beautifully with the early peonies, bearded irises, and tulips. These viburnums are deciduous flowering shrubs native to China, Korea, and Japan—the Latin word *plicatum* means "pleated," referring to the texture of the leaves. This species grows quite large—mine are about 10 feet (3 m) wide by 12 feet (3.6 m) high—so plenty of room is needed to accommodate the mature shrub. It takes years to grow but will flower in the first year or so after planting.

Opposite and above: A mixed arrangement can be impactful with just two types of flowers, as in this sparse, elegant pairing of viburnum (snipped from the bush right outside our living room) and 'Elizabeth' magnolia branches. Although the two make a wonderful foundation to support more tender blooms, this pared-down approach allows space for contemplation.

Lilies of the Valley

Though it's hard to name just one scent as a favorite, the lily of the valley's natural perfume sits squarely at the top of my list (perhaps along with roses and peonies). Also, I carried a bouquet of lilies of the valley (*Convallaria majalis*) when Wally and I were married in mid–May, so I have a strong connection to the plant. Before I had gardens of my own, I purchased the most delicate and tiny bunches of these at the flower market in Manhattan and would keep vases full of them at my bedside or on a dining table, where I could appreciate their beautiful aroma.

For these reasons, lily of the valley was one of the first flowers I planted in the round garden in Weston. Years later, it is funny to pull out huge clumps that would love to take over the beds completely. I happily give the roots away, though I always make sure to keep enough on hand.

Lily of the valley is a rhizomatous perennial, part of the Asparagaceae family, native to Europe and Asia. Its small, hairy roots are planted just below the soil level. It does well in shade, but many of mine live in full sun and are perfectly happy. Once established, the roots can push out other plants, so constant editing is necessary to keep the underground growth in check. The plant is poisonous, meaning there's no threat of deer or other animals eating it.

I love to make short, squat vases to hold large bunches of tiny lily of the valley. The blossoms also work well with any of the other May flowers, including peonies, lilacs, and violets.

I made this ruffled porcelain bisque pedestal vase to showcase the tiny florets of lily of the valley. For a whimsical display, I laid the delicate cuttings down lengthwise and added a few fern fronds at the base and forget-me-nots on top.

Bleeding Hearts

The tiny petals that form the perennial flower known as bleeding heart (*Dicentra spectabilis*) are truly a wonder. The specific epithet, *spectabilis*, means "spectacular" or "showy." The common name is derived from the exerted inner petals "bleeding" from the outer petals, each of which is shaped like a heart, with gorgeous inner and outer colors (commonly pink and white, but purple and black varieties exist as well). I'm continually delighted by the way the heads sway on the stem and are arranged in graduated sizes.

Bleeding hearts are native to Siberia, Japan, northern China, and Korea. The flowers are typically found in moist grasslands or shady forests. The bleeding hearts on our property were planted by previous owners. The first year we moved in, I discovered several bushes living in the shade of the maple tree. Now, when the bleeding hearts appear in spring, I feel true joy. They continue to bloom for several months; by midsummer, the foliage dies back. If planting in a border, it is best to place later-blooming plants such as ferns, hostas, or perennial begonias adjacent to bleeding hearts, to cover the empty spot by the end of summer. Nonetheless, this delicate-looking plant returns reliably every year and blooms nicely in partial or full shade, with minimal maintenance. Bleeding hearts are not fussy—a spot with good organic soil out of the strong sun is all they need.

Once cut, bleeding hearts last well in a vase. It's best to cut the stems long and strip away the lower leaves. For a mixed arrangement, I like to set them first, as their stems are strong and provide a good support system for the other flowers; generally, I pair bleeding hearts with lilacs, tulips, daffodils, and early peonies. I also save a few stems to place in the arrangement at the end, to highlight their heart-shaped flowers.

Opposite: The graceful stems of bleeding heart guide the eye through this arrangement of mixed daffodils.

Below: This clump of bleeding heart growing in our yard happily returns each spring.

LEAVING A GARDEN IN BLOOM

Stepping away from the garden is never easy, least of all when some of the flowers are at the height of their spectacular beauty. No matter how long I will be away, I always go into a bit of a panic before I leave. If the tulips, lilacs, and azaleas are blooming, I fear that they will be finished before I return. And there are other garden chores to consider as well. If I am gone in May, for example, how will the dahlia tubers get planted?

Last year, when I returned from a ten-day trip in June, I found that chaos had ensued. (It is especially hard to keep things on track that month.) The mint was invading most of the raised beds on the old tennis court; despite my spending a week pulling out as much as possible, the roots are still lurking under the soil and will likely never be entirely eradicated. The zinnias that I planted in haste before leaving needed to be pinched back, and the roses, which were blooming spectacularly when I left, had finished their first flush and needed to be deadheaded and fertilized.

At the same time, the first dahlia bed that I had planted looked like a wasteland. I anticipated finding many of the robust old tubers getting ready to bloom, but what I saw instead were nubs barely out of the ground, with leaves mostly eaten by slugs. With no one around to monitor them, those slimy invaders had a field day with the young plants.

While traveling, I observed a community garden run on the biodynamic principles of Rudolf Steiner. The gardeners used plastic garden cloches to create a ring around fragile young plants, to keep snails and slugs from attacking. The cloches aren't particularly attractive, and I'm not thrilled about the use of plastic, but I quickly ordered a stack and placed them around the tubers. Fortunately, these rings did the trick; the plants recovered in time to be in fine bloom by August.

Another year, I was in London for a three-week trunk show during September, the height of dahlia season. Although the garden was watered in my absence so that plants stayed alive, the essential daily maintenance of deadheading, pruning, and staking did not happen, and I found mayhem upon my return. I did the best that I could to set things to rights; however, traveling is certainly a trade-off.

Yet I find that no matter how difficult it seems to tear myself away from the garden at peak bloom time, leaving even briefly provides a necessary shift in perspective. By observing other gardens, I'm inspired by new ideas and strategies. After an absence, I appreciate my own garden with fresh eyes. Even though there may be more work when I return, I don't regret my time away, as there is always next year and the promise of a new foray.

Roses

The subject of roses is almost as vast as their appeal. I know that I am not alone in finding myself captivated by this flower's exquisite variety of forms, range of colors and scales and shapes, enchanting aroma, fragile petals—all of it—in the garden and in the vase. I've been growing roses for about twenty-five years in my garden, arranging them in pots of all shapes and sizes in my studio, and photographing the blooms through all their stages, inspired by photographs by Edward Steichen and Tina Modotti, among others.

When I look for new roses to add to the garden, I take into account their history, especially if they're old rose varieties. I like to imagine the roses that were blooming at the same time as the ancient terra-cotta that I study. Roses are indeed mystical and ancient; their cultivation is believed to have begun more than five thousand years ago in China. Rose gardens were created at the time of the Roman Empire and are traced through the medieval period to the seventeenth century. In the late eighteenth century, the repeat-blooming rose was cultivated in Europe, with hybrid roses introduced from China. Napoléon's wife, Joséphine, designed a large rose collection at the Château de Malmaison in the early 1800s, with more than five hundred distinct species.

Though I consider roses an essential flower for my arrangements, it has taken me years to understand how to grow them well. Even now, when the bushes explode with flowers each June, I am thrilled at their beauty and a bit surprised, frankly, that they bloomed at all. When I first planted roses, I mainly worried that the August humidity in Connecticut would impede their growth. Initially, I placed the old roses in the round garden. They survived, despite my inexperience, and went on to provide the most gorgeously perfumed moments while in bloom. Among those early endeavors in growing roses, a few varieties stand out: 'Constance Spry', 'Charles de Mills', and an old apothecary rose, which all opened beautifully in deep shades of pink and fuchsia.

Over time, the short bloom windows of the old roses were simply not enough to satisfy my fixation; I wanted roses from season to season, for as long as I could grow them. Thankfully, the David Austin varieties that repeatedly bloom were a good point of entry into this world. I started putting bare-root roses in the shallow beds on the tennis court garden, where they thrived, much to my amazement. It turns out they love the dry heat of the court surface. I made sure to use metal supports to help hold the rose branches together as they grew.

I adore everything about 'Sally Holmes' roses: the single-petal form, creamy white petals, and saffron-colored stamens. Here the flowers are combined in a pyramid-style tulipiere with annual pale peach asters, fennel flowers, tuberoses, pink Japanese anemones, and dahlias.

'Veilchenblau'
'Ausencart' (Benjamin Britten)
'Weksproulses' (Honey Dijon)

'Ausdecorum' (Darcey Bussell)
'Meijecycka' (Limoncello)
'Distant Drums'

'Constance Spry'
'Ausnyson' (Lady of Shalott)
'Wekmerewby' (Grande Dame)

'Belle de Crécy'
'Sally Holmes'
'Bathsheba'

'Belinda's Blush'
'Variegata di Bologna'
'Ausbrother' (Lady Emma Hamilton)

'Auseasel' (Vanessa Bell)
'Ausbaker' (Teasing Georgia)
'Thérèse Bugnet'

Two years ago, because I was running out of room in the beds themselves, I ordered about twenty-five different types of roses to place in 20-inch (51 cm) flowerpots alongside the raised beds. I placed a few terra-cotta shards in the bottom of each pot for drainage and airflow before I filled in with a combination of potting soil and manure. These newest additions, in colors ranging from pale cream to yellow to the deepest of reds, have greatly increased my options for arrangements and bring me much joy when they're in bloom.

HOW TO GROW ROSES

Rosebushes need airflow and space, as well as fertilizer a few times throughout the growing season. Drip irrigation in the garden beds is important to keep the roots adequately (but not overly) watered. I water the roses in the pots by hand, taking care not to douse from overhead, which can encourage fungal disease. Early in spring, the roses are fertilized with a fresh layer of organic manure, a practice I repeat again in mid-June and early September.

All roses need some kind of support. I find that the metal pyramid towers work best in the raised beds; I place the towers alongside the rosebushes and loosely tie biodegradable garden string around both. For the roses in pots, I install four or five branches around the perimeter of the pot to form a teepee shape, which I secure with string at the top and around the base of the branches as needed.

My gardening friends taught me that the best time to prune rosebushes is when the forsythia is in bloom, which is when the roses are just starting to bud. If rose branches are cut too early in spring, the pruning encourages new growth that could be damaged by an unexpected cold snap. I also hand-till the soil around the roots of each plant, to check for any suckers (errant canes that grow from the rootstock of the rosebush) that might appear, which can kill off the rose itself. Sometimes suckers develop if the grafted rose above the rootstock has died; other times it's a mystery why they appear. If a rosebush dies, I pull it out and plant a new bare-root rose. If the sucker and rose are growing at the same time, I cut the sucker very close to the root ball so that it doesn't sap nutrients from the main rose and compromise the blooms.

Because my garden is organic, I do not use pesticides to battle the beetles, aphids, and other pests that regularly prey on my roses. Instead, I drop the beetles into a jar of water to drown them and wash the aphids off with soapy water. My friend Connie Quesada taught me a solution to treat the roses: If a leaf begins to discolor and turn yellow, pull it off and dispose of it in a bin that is kept separate from the garden compost, to prevent it from contaminating the soil.

Every year, my goal is to cultivate roses in as many colors and forms as I possibly can. When the range of varieties comes into bloom in June, the fragrance in the garden—and in any room where the blossoms are placed—is nothing short of spectacular.

HOW TO ARRANGE ROSES

I am not strict about where I cut rose stems from the bush. I usually cut above a leaf branch that gives the stem a nice length for whichever vase I have chosen to use. I strip the lower stems of leaves and cut off the thorns, if they are particularly large. Freshly cut roses usually last three or four days in a vase. They can be massed together, with any other flower, or displayed simply as one stem with a perfect bloom. I save the petals after they fall off the bud to use in jams and jellies (see page 111 for a favorite recipe), to garnish cakes, or simply to put in bowls for fragrance.

The first group of co-bloomers that pair well with roses are the bearded irises, peonies, and late-blooming tulips. Next come the lilies, larkspurs, and poppies. Roses that bloom repeatedly can be arranged with zinnias, dahlias, cosmos, asters, and other fall flowers and foliage.

FAVORITE VARIETIES

***Rosa* 'Ausbernard' (Munstead Wood)**
A repeat bloomer with deep purple-red petals and a strong old-rose fragrance

R. 'Ausencart' (Benjamin Britten) An orange-red that is the best color for arrangements, especially with blue flowers

R. 'Ausnyson' (Lady of Shalott) A deep orange David Austin rose with yellow overtones and a chalice cup shape

R. 'Auswest' (Carding Mill) A lovely scented apricot-yellow repeat-blooming David Austin rose

R. 'Charles de Mills' A single-blooming deep fuchsia flat multipetaled old rose with an incredible perfume

R. 'Constance Spry' An old rose that blooms once, with a deep pink cupped head and strong fragrance

R. 'Sally Holmes' A single white rose with many blooms on a stem that flower all summer

When I pulled these small terra-cotta vases out of the kiln, it was the prime moment of the first rose bloom. I seized the opportunity to showcase the vases and flowers together.

QUINCE JELLY WITH ROSE PETALS

The best part about this recipe, which is a variation of one in the *River Cottage Preserves Handbook* by Pam Corbin, is that it doesn't require a specific measurement of fruit. The quince is first boiled to soften the flesh, and then strained, at which point the syrup is combined with sugar to make the jelly.

In September, I dried the deep red Munstead Wood roses; the petals held their color beautifully even when submerged in the jelly. One important note: Make sure to use rose petals that have been grown organically; anything else may contain pesticides or other chemicals that are unsafe for eating. *Makes 10 to 12 half-pint (240 ml) jars*

7 or 8 ripe quinces (3 to 4 pounds/1.5 to 2 kg) or apples (about 8 pounds/3.5 kg)
About ½ cup (7 g) dried organic rose petals
Sugar
Juice of 2 lemons

SPECIAL EQUIPMENT
10 to 12 half-pint (240 ml) sterilized canning jars with lids, kept hot
A pot large enough to process
Basic canning equipment

Wash and chop the fruit, including the skins and cores. Place the pieces in a large pot and cover with water by about an inch (2.5 cm). Add 10 to 12 rose petals. Cut a round of parchment paper to the circumference of your pot, then place it in the pot to keep the quinces submerged.

Bring to a boil over medium-high heat, then reduce the heat to medium-low and simmer until the quince flesh is soft, an hour or a bit longer. Pour the quince and petals into a sieve set over a large bowl, and let the mixture drain for several hours or overnight.

Measure the poaching liquid. For every cup of liquid, measure ¾ cup (150 g) of sugar. Pour the quince liquid back into the pot and add the sugar and lemon juice. Bring the sugar mixture to a boil and continue boiling over medium-low heat until the mixture reaches 220°F (104°C). Though it may take longer for the jelly to reach the right consistency by cooking over medium-low heat, the flavor will be better if it's not cooked at a high temperature. If you don't have a thermometer, use the plate test to gauge when the jelly is finished (see Note).

Let the jelly cool slightly, then ladle it into the hot sterilized jars, leaving ½ inch (1.5 cm) of headspace. Place a couple of rose petals on top of the jelly in each jar, then gently push the petals under the surface to submerge them. Wipe the rims clean and carefully attach the lids. Follow the boiling-water-canning procedure (see the USDA guidelines at nchfp.uga.edu/resources) to process the jars for 10 minutes, adjusting for altitude as needed per USDA guidelines.

Note: If you don't have a thermometer, put a plate in the freezer before you begin making the jelly. Place a teaspoon of the boiling syrup on the plate and return to the freezer for a few minutes. If the jelly gets a skin when pushed with a finger, it's ready.

PART III

AESTIVAL

SPANNING FROM MID-JUNE THROUGH MID-AUGUST in the northern hemisphere, aestival (the Latin term for summer) is close to but not quite the same as the three months we recognize as summer on the traditional calendar. During this period, which is considered the most vibrant time for both plants and animals, the garden changes dramatically. The sun is strong, and the days—and shadows—are long. Work schedules are looser and more carefree than at other times of year, which allows for more time tending to the garden.

I take care to pinch the dahlias, zinnias, and asters to encourage them to branch and produce more flowers when they appear in a few weeks' time, and to pull out any extraneous volunteers and "weeds" that are taking up too much room. I also cut back the daffodil and tulip leaves, plant more annuals in the empty spaces, and cut back the roses after their first bloom to encourage a second in early fall. Many of the flowers that bloom in this season seem to stretch toward the sun. Some are tall and lanky, with all manner of petal formations—from wispy and ethereal poppies to sturdy and showy lilies. Others climb up trellises and over fences to capture the brighter sun before opening in beautiful bursts. Multiple herbs flower at this time as well, showcasing their appeal beyond the kitchen and going straight into the vase.

Poppies

This beautiful flower is an herbaceous perennial, meaning it emerges in early spring and then its leaves and stems die back after its bloom time in summer. I have planted a few perennial poppies in the garden and particularly love the color of 'Patty's Plum'.

I have discovered annual poppies that come in the most delicate sherbet colors and fantastic petal shapes, perfect for photographing in my bud vases. I choose breadseed, pompon, silk, and champagne varieties and keep many of the arrangements simple, so that the gorgeous petals can be seen clearly.

Some gardeners suggest searing the ends of poppy stems once cut, before putting them in a vase. In my experience, this doesn't seem to affect the life of the flower, so I don't usually do this. If poppies are left in a cool area of the house and out of the direct sun, they can last for a week or two.

It is always a thrill to plant poppy seeds in the middle of winter because they are a promise of flowers to come in June. They need cold weather to facilitate germination, so I find it is easiest to direct-seed them around late February, even if there is snow on the ground. I put the tiny seeds in a bucket with potting soil, which helps disperse them, then dribble the soil-seed mixture along the snow. I also order plugs, as I like to have backup in case for some reason my seeds do not germinate correctly.

Poppies do not like to be moved once the seed has set roots, so I plant them on the edge of the beds where they won't be disturbed when I begin to put in the annuals and dahlia tubers. At this point, I can't see where the natives and perennials will emerge in April, but I have a loose memory of their location. A random approach means I am in for a few surprises come spring and summer. And besides, poppy seeds are sturdy. They will find their way around the other flowers. If we are lucky, maybe they will be joined by a few volunteer poppies from last year's seeds as well. The more, the merrier.

Among peonies, roses, bearded irises, foxgloves, elderflowers, deep blue nigellas, and tulips, two scarlet, papery Oriental poppies grab the focus; their black centers are in keeping with the black background of the photo.

FAVORITE VARIETIES

Papaver rhoeas **'Amazing Grey'** An annual poppy with fragile gray-lavender petals

P. somniferum With 2- to 4-foot-tall (0.6 to 1.2 m) stems, flower heads with large petals in pastel shades, and large pods that can be dried and whose seeds can be used for baking; commonly known as the breadseed poppy

P. somniferum **'Danish Flag'** A large scarlet bloom with a white cross of color in the center

P. somniferum **'Lilac Pompon'** Frilly double and semidouble flowers in pastel shades

'Patty's Plum' Oriental poppy
'Hungarian Blue' breadseed poppy

Corn poppy
'Prince of Orange' Oriental poppy

'White Frills' breadseed poppy
'Mother of Pearl' corn poppy

'Purple Peony' breadseed poppy
'Scarlet Peony' breadseed poppy

Annual Shirley poppies thrive in the tennis court raised beds. Here they are displayed in one of my classic Phoebe vases along with roses, borage, nigella, and an early-blooming dahlia.

Flowering Vines and Climbers

Cup and Saucer Vine, Hyacinth Bean, Clematis, Passionflower,
Morning Glory, Nasturtium, Sweet Pea

Vines and climbers may not be the first plants that come to mind when you think about cutting gardens, but I grow a range of flowers in this category, not only for the beautiful colors and texture they bring while they ramble about the garden but also for their distinct character in arrangements.

I love the way that vines and climbers beautifully blur lines when I want them to; in the garden, that means covering up the necessary fencing, and in the vase, hiding where the edge of the vase meets some of the taller flowers within it. A few, such as clematis, are perennial, but most are annuals that I plan for each season, waiting until the chance of frost has passed (usually by mid-May) to plant them.

Over the years, I have collected trellises and metal towers to support these flowers; I appreciate the height that the architectural elements give to both gardens year-round as well. As the vines climb, I tie them with biodegradable string to encourage them to wrap around the support. Often I'll collect branches that have fallen on the property to use as additional support structures, especially if they are nice and tall, with lots of opportunity for draping.

The Chelsea Physic Garden in London, one of the oldest botanical gardens in England, has been my longtime source of inspiration for these plants. Each time I visit, I make sure to check out which vines are in bloom, and to photograph the supports the gardeners have set up for each so that I can try to replicate them when I get back home.

CUP AND SAUCER VINE

I love the striking profile of *Cobaea scandens*, more commonly known as cup and saucer vine (due to the shape of its blossoms; other names include cathedral bells or monastery bells). The colors of the tendrils and flower heads are difficult to describe, kind of a mix of purple, lavender, and chartreuse. Native to Mexico, the plant is not winter hardy, but I persist in trying to grow it every year here in Connecticut, with moderate success. Some seasons are more favorable than others. The vine doesn't like to be

Cup and saucer vines trail out of a marbleized, three-spouted vase. Hyacinth beans, coleus leaves (and their flower spires), strawflowers, and wine-red dahlias reinforce the maroon and purple palette. White Japanese anemones provide the staccato note.

'Jackmanii' clematis
'Rooguchi' clematis
'Blue Celeste' sweet pea

'Grandpa Ott' morning glory
Trailing nasturtium mix
Purple hyacinth bean

'Inspiration' passionflower
Passionflower × *alato-caerulea*
Cup and saucer vine

too damp or crowded. According to the information on the seed packet, it's a fast grower in full sun, but mine seemed happiest on the tennis court in a bed that gets some afternoon shade. One winter, I kept a cup and saucer plant in the greenhouse until it was warm enough to return outside, which worked out quite well. I find growing the vines worth the challenges they pose, as I like to study their distinctive forms in the garden, and just one or two blooms add great impact to a mixed arrangement.

HYACINTH BEAN

I use cut hyacinth bean (*Lablab purpureus*) in an arrangement when I'm looking for something to wind its way down the length of a pedestal. The plant has a firm, rich reddish-purple stem, an abundance of gorgeous dark green leaves, and beautiful, bright-hued flowers. Thomas Jefferson loved the purple hyacinth bean, which was noted in his garden around 1804. The seeds are available at the Monticello website (along with lots of other historic flower and vegetable seeds).

I directly sow these annual vines in late April, in a spot that runs along the fence in my round garden. Though the lavender flowers turn into deep purple pods, they are ornamental and not to be confused with edible beans (in fact, they are believed to be toxic). I could save the beans in the pods to use the following spring, when it is time to plant the vine again, but I usually purchase fresh

seeds instead, to guarantee that there will be enough of that bloom to use in arrangements.

The deer seem to love the purple hyacinth bean as much as I do. This year, as the plants grew on the outside of the fence, the deer ate them down to nubs. It is hard to keep track of the plant material around the garden, but if I miss spraying with organic deer repellent such as Plantskydd, the hyacinth bean vine is doomed.

CLEMATIS

I learned about clematis, the so-called queen of the climbers, from my friend Kaye Heafey, who founded Chalk Hill Farm in Healdsburg, California, about twenty-five years ago. Kaye was a real groundbreaker in growing vines for the cut flower trade, and she had the most exquisite and healthy clematis. She also

FAVORITE CLEMATIS VARIETIES

Clematis tangutica Small, delicate yellow bells on a strong climbing vine; often called golden clematis

C. virginiana A native vine with dense clusters of small but showy white flowers

C. 'Betty Corning' Pale lavender blooms with bronze-tinted dark leaves

C. 'Etoile Violette' Dark purple, delicate flowers that will rebloom if pruned after first flowering

C. 'Jackmanii' A large purple-blue flower that's among the most popular and fast-growing clematis

C. 'Rooguchi' Nodding dark purple flowers that continue to bloom until the first frost

wrote a wonderful book on the subject, *A Celebration of Clematis: From the Gardens of Chalk Hill Nursery*, which I keep on hand for reference.

I once read that these perennials like to keep their heads in the sun and their feet in the shade. I order the plugs online, and then place them in spots in both gardens where there is plenty of ground cover around the roots. I look forward to seeing their shoots appear in early April, at which point I trim off the vines from the previous growing season. I go slowly and take care not to prune too much, since sometimes these have new shoots coming in as well. When the clematis blooms in June, I cut the flowers with their long tendrils, so they can fall out of the vase or bowl as the last additions.

PASSIONFLOWER

The form of each passionflower (genus *Passiflora*) is extraordinary: up to 3 inches (7.5 cm) across, with the majority having five sepals, five petals, a ring of radial filaments, five stamens, and an ovary of three carpels. The plant produces fantastic tendrils that are themselves works of art, as well as fruit that ostensibly symbolizes Christ's crown of thorns and his suffering, which helps explain the origin of the flower's name.

I first saw a passionflower plant blooming at gardener Tony Elliott's Snug Harbor Farm in Kennebunk, Maine, several years ago. It looks exotic and tropical, as if it belongs in Southeast Asia,

The stripes of this blue-and-white cobalt vase echo the vivid purple markings of the centers and petals of the passionflower. The trailing vines were too beautiful to cut, so I draped them around the vase.

though it is native to the southeastern United States, Mexico, and Central and South America.

Whenever I plant perennial passionflower vines among the roses and dahlias, I know that they will wrap themselves around their neighboring friends, so I keep a close eye to ensure they don't smother the underlying flowers. I prune the vine to keep it in check. If I am organized in fall (which is not always the case), I dig up and pot the passionflower before the frosts come and winter it in the greenhouse, because it will not survive the cold. I bring it outside in May, when I plant other annuals and dahlia tubers.

In the studio, I use the passionflower in a vase by itself or add it to a larger mixed arrangement at the end, so that the exquisite flowers are prominently on view.

MORNING GLORY

The twining vine known as morning glory (*Ipomoea purpurea*) is an annual. Once it has been planted, however, it will reseed just about anywhere it pleases. (When not trained to climb up a support structure, the plant can serve as a ground cover.) In early April, I direct-sow it against the fence. When the vines return the next year, however, they inevitably reappear elsewhere, often in the center of a garden bed or the compost pile. It's not exactly where I wish them to grow, but I don't bother to pull the volunteers out.

I admire the morning glory's vigorous growing habit, either in full sun or shade. It seems to be happy in any soil and is deer-proof as well.

I consider the morning glory's dark blue flowers an essential component of my summer arrangements (though they come in many other colors, including white, pink, pale blue, and deep violet). I love to weave the stems in and out of the other flowers in a vase. The plant's common name comes from the belief that the flowers only bloom on the vine in the morning, which is true, but even if the bloom fades, other buds on the same stem will open the next day. Sometimes I have pulled a cut vine out of a vase, left it on the floor, and observed that the flowers keep opening on their own anyway.

NASTURTIUM

Years ago, when Wally and I were staying at a hotel in northern California, I marveled at nasturtiums that were growing around the property. It was November, and the vines and their brightly colored flowers were draped over every piece of ground and hillside, which surprised me at that time of year. In Connecticut, this annual flower (also a culinary herb) would have been long gone once the hard frost hit.

Whether planted as a vine or as ground cover, nasturtiums are very easy to grow and can be directly seeded in May, once any chance of frost has passed.

In general, I opt for bright yellow, orange, and red nasturtiums and often choose an organic mix from Johnny's Selected Seeds, particularly *Tropaeolum minus* 'Jewel Mix' and 'Alaska Mix', which have great foliage. Among my absolute favorite varieties is the classic cultivar 'Empress of India'. I also purchase the plants in pots from a local nursery, as I prefer to have a backup for my efforts. Nasturtiums like full sun and lots of air around them while they establish themselves. They are happier in cooler weather and should keep growing even as temperatures drop at night in the fall months.

Once they are in bloom, I cut the vines long for flower arrangements and usually place them in a vase first, then layer other flowers on top. I love the peppery taste of the leaves and petals in salads, too; the name originates from the Latin *nas* (or "nose," for the spicy smell and taste of the leaves and petals) and *tortum* (or "twist," for the way they grow).

SWEET PEA

When I started to expand my flower repertoire to ensure that something was always in bloom throughout the growing months, sweet peas (*Lathyrus odoratus*) were one of the first seeds that I ordered. I admired how the English grew them so beautifully, and I yearned to have a plentiful, fragrant bunch of my own. Each year, around St. Patrick's Day, I sow the seeds outside (about 1 inch/2.5 cm or so into the soil) into a few large

FAVORITE SWEET PEA VARIETIES

Lathyrus odoratus **'Blue Ripple'** Long stems and lightly ruffled petals marked by the prettiest shade of lavender-blue

L. odoratus **'Mammoth Mix'** Large flowers in a wide range of colors, with extra-long stems and a sweet scent

L. odoratus **'Midnight'** Beautifully deep maroon frilly flowers that make a bold statement in an arrangement

L. odoratus **'Spencer Ripple Mix'** A British beauty with an incredibly sweet fragrance and ethereal bicolor petals

designated flowerpots on the tennis court garden, with branches in place to support the tendrils that emerge in late April. To ensure that I will indeed have plenty of sweet peas to cut when June rolls around, I also purchase plugs to augment the seedlings, usually a mix (Johnny's Selected Seeds has a nice one called 'Royal Mix') to increase my options for arrangements, plus a few exquisite specialty sweet peas (see the list above).

Once blooming, sweet peas should be harvested regularly to encourage more shoots. The vine and flowers prefer partial shade in the afternoon and like to be well watered, though not overly so.

When I'm arranging, I reserve the sweet peas for my petite bouquets so that they aren't lost in larger, more exuberant groupings. Or I display them by themselves so that their singular forms, combined with their inimitable fragrance, get full attention.

LENTIL SALAD WITH NASTURTIUMS

Because I begin working in the studio so early in the morning, by lunchtime I am famished. This means I try to make things ahead so that something tasty is ready and waiting for me when I take a break. One batch of this hearty salad can keep me going for a few days. If I have guests for lunch, I fold nasturtium flowers and leaves into the lentils and sprinkle a few over the top just before serving. The bright orange blossoms make the table look fresh and cheery, and the leaves are wonderfully peppery. *Serves 4 to 6*

1 cup (150 g) French green lentils, picked over and rinsed
1 sprig fresh rosemary
1 small shallot, finely chopped
1 garlic clove, finely chopped
½ cup (120 ml) olive oil, plus more as needed
¼ cup (60 ml) balsamic or white wine vinegar, plus more as needed

Juice of ½ lemon
2 teaspoons Dijon mustard
½ cup (25 g) sun-dried tomatoes, chopped
½ cup (45 g) walnuts, toasted
Coarse salt and freshly ground black pepper
1 cup (25 g) nasturtium leaves and flowers, quartered if large (reserve a few whole ones for garnish)

In a saucepan, combine the lentils with 2½ cups (590 ml) water and add the rosemary. Bring to a boil, then cover and reduce the heat to low. Simmer just until the lentils are tender and firm, not mushy, 15 to 20 minutes; do not overcook. Drain the lentils and let cool.

In a salad bowl, combine the shallot and garlic. Whisk in the oil, vinegar, lemon juice, and mustard to make a dressing. Add the lentils, tomatoes, and walnuts, tossing to combine. Season to taste with salt and pepper.

Gently fold in most of the nasturtium leaves and flowers. Taste and adjust the salt, pepper, oil, or vinegar, if necessary, before garnishing with whole leaves and flowers and serving.

Lilies

From my earliest days as a gardener, I have planted lilies of all kinds. If protected by fencing, many of them return faithfully year after year. For my growing region, the first varieties open in mid-June. By having multiple varieties with different bloom times, I can have new ones continually through September.

Years ago, I was captivated by an image of a 'Star Gazer' lily in the photography collection at the Getty Museum in Los Angeles. What I thought was a photograph was a hand-colored collotype by the Japanese artist Ogawa Kazumasa. The image has a haunting late-nineteenth-century quality, and I was drawn to it because I grow the same variety of lily in my garden. When I made the arrangement in the photo opposite, I was referencing Ogawa Kazumasa's colors and simplicity. I purchased a reprint of his book *Some Japanese Flowers*, originally published in 1896, and often study the blooms that he selected.

Lilies, depending on the supplier, are offered both in fall and spring. (See the list on page 134 for some of my favorites.) Note that Asiatic and Oriental lilies, such as 'Casa Blanca', may need to go an entire year before reaching full bloom.

HOW TO GROW LILIES

Bulbs, depending on the size/height of the flower to come, are planted 6 to 8 inches (15 to 20 cm) deep to support the stem. Often the tallest varieties need to be staked or tied with string once they reach 4 to 6 feet (122 to 183 cm) for additional bracing. Lily bulbs need full sun, and I fertilize them with fish emulsion at the same time as the dahlias. They are usually plagued by red lily beetles that show up as early as March. (These bugs also love fritillary stalks.) My strategy is to quickly pick the leaf they are resting on and squish the bugs on the ground. If it is a particularly bad

A small, ash-glazed vase holds numerous stems of 'Star Gazer' lily; it is astounding to see how closely they resemble the lilies in Ogawa Kazumasa's collotype (below). Flowers transcend time and link together different moments forever.

Lily.

Lily, Ogawa Kazumasa, 1896.

Majestic and grand *Lilium regale* stems stand tall in
the raised beds; once cut, a huge array of blooms is
displayed in a wood-fired, ash-glazed tulipiere.

year, I will spray with Safer organic bug spray. If I've missed the bugs and their black larvae appear on the bottom side of the lily leaves, I merely sweep my gloved hand up the stem and remove the unpleasant slime.

HOW TO ARRANGE LILIES

Lilies can be cut while the buds are closed and then placed in water, where they will bloom gradually. They have a splendidly long flowering time. When I have my pottery exhibition in North Haven, Maine, at the end of every July, I cut most of the unopened tiger and 'Casa Blanca' lilies from my gardens and put them in buckets filled with water in the car. If the buds start to open by the time I have moved into the gallery, usually a few days later, I know that they will last the week of the show. The lily-filled vases throughout the gallery, especially those with the scented 'Casa Blanca' types, make a dramatic presentation.

Lilies are magnificent on their own, of course, but they also work well in an arrangement of other blooms such as roses, peonies, zinnias, dahlias, delphiniums, hydrangeas, and apple tree branches. Their stems are sturdy and tall. I strip off the lower leaves that would be below the water in a vase. Some years, I have to quickly throw a tall vase form to accommodate the height and weight of the stems! I occasionally display lilies in one of my tulipieres.

Lilium henryi Often called Henry's lily or tiger lily, a native of China with downward-facing, speckled orange petals; they work well arranged on their own or as a focal point in a mixed bouquet

L. lancifolium 'Flore Pleno' The double tiger lily, so named for its striking spotted black-and-orange petals

L. regale One of my favorite lilies to photograph on their own, thanks to their huge pink-and-white petals and extra-long golden yellow filaments

L. 'African Queen' Giant cheerful blooms in a range of oranges, from apricot to dark melon, with a pinkish-purplish reverse

L. 'Black Beauty' A stunning near-black (actually deep dark raspberry) flower with lots of buds per stem

L. 'Casa Blanca' Enormous, pure white, gorgeously fragrant, and irresistible Oriental lilies

L. 'Golden Splendor' A quintessential trumpet lily, with an intoxicating scent and huge, deep yellow petals and maroon striping on the reverse

L. 'Lady Alice' A sturdy, reliable, resplendent variation on a Turk's cap lily, with warm swaths of orange and yellow atop large white petals

L. 'Star Gazer' Among the most common and beloved lilies with hot pink petals tinged white at the edges and a remarkable fragrance

Henry's lily
'Black Beauty'

'Golden Splendor'
Tiger lily

Fantastic Spires

Verbascum, Allium, Foxglove, Delphinium, Nigella,
Snapdragon, Hollyhock, Larkspur

Wherever I can find space between the dahlias, bearded irises, roses, and lilies in the garden beds, I plant alliums, delphiniums, foxgloves, hollyhocks, larkspurs, nigellas, snapdragons, and verbascums. It simply wouldn't be summer in my garden without them. I don't have masses of these flowers, just enough to provide a formal or colorful accent to an arrangement. Their presence adds to the overall exuberance and spontaneous aspect of the raised beds, and in the vase, they offer height and drama.

In this arrangement, the deep red centers of the tiny verbascum flowers pick up similar tones in the petals of the hollyhocks, foxgloves, and one 'Charles de Mills' rose. All are held in place by a flower pin in a pewter-glazed vase.

VERBASCUM

I was given my first verbascum plants by my friend Page Dickey, and I think of her every time I see them blooming robustly. No matter how early I go out to visit the verbascums in the morning, the bumblebees and honeybees have beaten me to them. I watch the insects happily buzzing from floret to floret. Plants in the *Verbascum* genus are considered perennial or biennial, but mine self-seed, so I always have a nice selection of the yellow and creamy white varieties in the round garden. I also grow the peach-colored cultivar 'Helen Johnson' in the beds on the tennis court.

Verbascum's other common name is mullein; it is part of the Scrophulariaceae family and related to the great mullein (*V. thapsus*), the large yellow wild species one sees growing on the side of the road or springing up uninvited in the garden. The flower is much loved by the butterflies as well as the bees, so I leave the volunteers where they emerge and cut down the huge stems after they finish blooming. My verbascums flower around the same time (mid-June) as the first lilies, roses, and late peonies, and I love to group them together in a vase.

ALLIUM

I find alliums amusing. The easy-to-grow flowers function as exclamation points in the garden generally from the middle of May through mid-July, around the same time as the late-blooming peonies, verbascums, and lady's mantle. Inspired by their presence in two important English gardens, Hadspen (which has since morphed into another garden) and Sissinghurst (see page 279), I added a few alliums to my own garden. Their heads stand out dramatically just when the early-summer-blooming flowers are starting to gain height. If left standing in the garden beyond their bloom time, the heads dry naturally and make wonderfully sculptural elements as the season progresses.

All varieties of allium bulbs can be planted in large groups in autumn, at the same time as the tulips, either in rows (down an allée, for example) or mixed between shrubs and other flowers. I plant the bulbs abundantly on the periphery of my garden beds, since I grow them for cutting and don't wish to interfere with planting my dahlia tubers. Many of the alliums seed in the cracks and base of the raised beds on the old tennis court, and the bees are absolutely mad for them. As much I would like to thin them, I surrender and just leave them for the insect population to enjoy.

If unsupported by surrounding plants or bamboo stakes, alliums may flop

FAVORITE ALLIUM VARIETIES

Allium cristophii The star of Persia, with spectacularly large (8- to 10-inch/20 to 25 cm) globes, each with fifty starry florets

A. schubertii Schubert's allium, an especially profuse and lush species, with more than a hundred florets

A. sphaerocephalon The drumstick allium, with an egg-shaped head and long, slender stem

Nectaroscordum siculum ssp. bulgaricum The Sicilian honey lily, an eccentric allium cousin marked by wide (about 4 inches/ 10 cm) umbels, with beautiful bell-shaped, deep tricolored (mauve, green, and white) florets

onto the ground when blooming rather than grow upright. The flower heads, composed of twenty to thirty beautifully striated pendants, have a peculiar skunk-like fragrance that I find oddly appealing (deer and other rodents are repelled by their smell, thankfully). I cut the stems of alliums as long as possible before adding them to an arrangement, so they can show above the fray.

FOXGLOVE

The common foxglove, or *Digitalis purpurea*, is native to Europe. It is a staple of English gardens. I have thought often of the most brilliant foxglove display I once saw at Rousham in Oxfordshire (see page 279), where the flowers were woven through the parterre garden next to the dovecote.

Foxgloves are an herbaceous biennial plant, meaning they grow from seeds the first year and bloom the next. The trick is to have foxglove seeds in rotation, so that some of the spires bloom each year. You can buy the plants in pots at a nursery, but chances are the flowers will come back the next year in a completely different color. These blossoms certainly have a mind of their own. I started out with foxgloves in the garden beds but they have since established themselves randomly elsewhere.

They show up in May and June, at the same time as the peonies, and I use them as accents in arrangements. (I wash my hands after harvesting and arranging the

  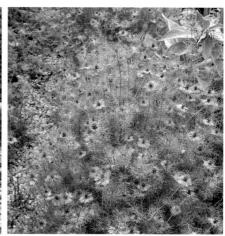

Star of Persia allium
'White Blush' verbascum
Common foxglove

'Potomac Pink' snapdragon
'Fancy Blue Purple' larkspur
'Henry VIII' hollyhock

Love-in-a-mist
'Helen of Troy' foxglove
'Magic Fountains Sky Blue' delphinium

flowers, since they are toxic to humans and animals.) The flowers last a fairly long time in the vase. As they age, the bottom florets fade, so you can pull them off and keep the rest.

I have been purchasing foxglove plants from The Bunker Farm in Vermont the past few years and have had good success with *Digitalis trojana* 'Helen of Troy', which has happily reseeded in the same sunny spot for the past few years. I also order most of the sustainably produced unusual varieties of seedlings that Bunker offers and look forward to seeing this year's offerings. (Bunker does not ship their products, unfortunately, but if you are in the Northeast, you can find them at various plant sales and also visit them directly to pick up your order. Wherever you live, I encourage you to find similar specialty growers in your region.)

DELPHINIUM

In some ways, I regard delphinium as my fantasy flower. It's one of the only true blue flowers in nature. I want to grow it successfully, but it's a challenge. Learning to cultivate delphiniums (genus *Delphinium*) remains a work in progress for me, and I usually buy new plants in spring. The few that grow in my raised beds yield flowers from June through September. Delphiniums are often blue and purple, in varying shades of intensity, but there are shades of pink and white as well.

About ten years ago, I had the opportunity to visit Les Jardins de Quatre-Vents, the garden created by the celebrated (and self-taught) horticulturist Francis Cabot on his family's property in La Malbaie, Quebec. Open to the public for just four days every summer, the garden is a breathtaking array of garden rooms. The flowers that I remember most were the giant delphiniums, which were planted in a long perennial border as well as the cutting garden. The stalks were easily 12 feet (3.5 m) tall and resplendent in blues and whites, and they were my inspiration for growing my own.

I was also inspired by the great photographer Edward Steichen (see page 72), who grew spectacular delphiniums just 5 miles (8 km) from where I live, in the town of Redding, Connecticut. If he could grow these beauties, I thought, then I would have to keep trying.

Matt Mattus, a master gardener in Worcester, Massachusetts, advises planting delphiniums on their own and not in the context of a mixed border. They require six to eight hours of full sun; rich, organic soil; and plenty of room and airflow around them. Delphiniums

FAVORITE DELPHINIUM VARIETIES

Delphinium **Belladonna Group** Dark blue beauties that produce secondary spikes in late summer

D. **Elatum Group** This group comes in violet, blue, pink, and/or white hues with dense, erect flowers

D. **Magic Fountains Series** A shorter variety in shades of blue, pink, and white

This arrangement's palette drew inspiration from the deep pink in the petals of the hollyhocks. Geranium flowers and leaves form the foundation, peeking out from beneath the roses, nigellas, carnations, poppies, and lilies.

are toxic to humans if eaten but are otherwise safe to cut and to handle.

NIGELLA

Nigellas are graceful, upright, happy arrivals to the midsummer garden party. I first noticed the annual *Nigella damascena* (also known as love-in-a-mist) when I visited Rosemary Verey's garden at Barnsley House in England in the late nineties. I was taken by the wispiness of the stems and the intensity of the flower's color in the garden, which worked to balance the more pastel flowers in the beds. The genus name *Nigella* comes from the Latin word for "black," which refers to the seeds in the center of the pod after the flower finishes blooming. It's always a surprise to see where these seeds self-sow around the garden. I love the deep blue color of 'Miss Jekyll Blue', but white nigella is equally beautiful. There is also the Persian Jewels Group— a mixture of shades of mauve, lavender, purple, rose, light blue, and white double flowers.

I buy nigellas as plugs or directly sow the seeds into the beds—always in full sun, as they don't like to be moved once planted. Seeds can be successively sown over the summer months to guarantee continual blooming. Leaving the flowers in the garden to dry will encourage the dried seeds to disperse. The stems and leaves make a great support system in a vase when arranging a large bouquet. Both the flowers and seed heads add wonderful texture and color accent to a bouquet.

SNAPDRAGON

Snapdragons were one of my mother's favorite flowers, so as an homage to her, I include these cheerful blooms in my annuals selection, along with zinnias, cosmos, and others. When I first started growing snapdragons in the round garden, they were offered in the more common pastel shades of pink, orange, and yellow. Now the flowers are available from many specialty growers, and one can do a deep dive into unusual colors.

Snapdragons are easy to grow from seed, but I don't have a great track record with keeping the seedlings alive, so I choose a better route and buy plugs instead. If the snapdragons grown in the raised beds reseed, which happens often, they are one of the earliest flowers blooming in spring (unlike the plugs that I plant, which flower several weeks later). They also don't mind the frost in late fall

FAVORITE SNAPDRAGON VARIETIES

Antirrhinum majus **'Appleblossom'** A bicolor (salmon pink and white) bloom

A. majus **'Black Prince'** A crimson-red flower with dark green leaves that reseeds nicely

A. majus **'Madame Butterfly Red'** An azalea type with dark burgundy double blooms

A. majus **'Orange Wonder'** Gorgeous orange-pink combination

A. majus **'Potomac Orange'** Especially lush pink-orange petals and persevere when most other annuals have been stopped by the cold.

Their needs aren't many in the garden beds, other than sun and good soil. I situate them on the bed edges so I can reach them easily. Occasionally, if a stalk starts to fall over, I will tie it to a bamboo stake. For arranging, I cut the long snapdragon stems before all the buds are open; the closed ones generally open after they have been placed in a vase with water. When I'm adding a snapdragon to a vase, I strip the leaves at the bottom of the stem and add it into the mix at the end so that the lovely flower form isn't hidden in the abundance. Snaps pair especially well with dahlias and zinnias.

HOLLYHOCK

I treat my hollyhocks (*Alcea rosea*) as short-lived perennials and choose new ones in spring. They are technically biennials, which means they flower the second year after sowing, so I make sure to have a continual rotation to ensure bloom the following season, too. I especially love it when the flowers volunteer around the tennis court garden, popping up unexpectedly in cracks in the asphalt. I gravitate to the single black and deep red varieties, though the double-ruffle sherbet colors are also hard to resist.

Hollyhocks prefer well-drained soil and full sun. They are happy against a warm garden wall and occasionally require staking. They do need a bit of

room to grow, so I put my plugs on the edges of the raised beds; if necessary, I tie them to the tomato cages that hold the dahlias. One flower stalk can grow 5 to 9 feet (1.5 to 2.7 m) tall, with flowers along the length. I use the flowers at the back of an arrangement to emphasize the height and admire the open faces of the petals.

LARKSPUR

Larkspur (reclassified as *Consolida ajacis* and *C. regalis*, but still sometimes sold as *Delphinium consolida*) is native to northern America and parts of Africa and has been cultivated since the sixteenth century in England, where the common name is believed to have originated. It refers to the flower's shape, which resembles the spur of a lark's claw. Larkspur blooms in a wider range of colors than delphinium, including salmon pink, indigo, purple, rose, and white shades.

I am more successful with larkspur than delphinium, and it often reseeds for the next year. I buy larkspur as plugs and plant them in the raised beds in early May if they haven't come back on their own. Like delphinium, larkspur is toxic to humans and animals.

Larkspur is one of the necessary flowers that I grow for arrangements. The tall spires are effective as accents; I strip off the leaves and usually add the flowers at the end, as a lovely finishing touch.

Flowering Herbs

Dill, Feverfew, Sage, Lavender, Borage, Verbena,
Chive Flower, Elderflower, Calendula

Throughout the growing seasons, my garden is graced with a nice variety of flowering herbs. Beyond their endless culinary uses, they are wonderful additions to mixed arrangements and are pollinator magnets as well. The easy-to-grow perennials such as lavender and feverfew return faithfully every year, and the annuals, including borage and calendula, are reliably low-maintenance. None of these plants are particularly fussy, beyond the basics of good organic soil, adequate (never too much) water, ample sunlight, and regular deadheading or pruning.

DILL

I plant dill (*Anethum graveolens*) every spring and look forward to its scent in the garden. *Anethum* comes from the Greek word *aneeson* or *aneeton*, which means "strong smelling." Dill is an annual herb, part of the Apiaceae family, along with fennel, lovage, and parsley, and has been used since ancient times in Ayurvedic medicine. Once cut, the herb makes a good foundation for arrangements; the acid-yellow color of the fronds pairs wonderfully with other herbs such as feverfew and calendula, both of which flower at the same moment. I also chop fresh dill to add to salads, soups, and stews. Dill likes full sun and good air and space around the plant. It should not be put into the beds too early; it's best to wait until the temperature is around 50°F (10°C) at night, as for basil, tomatoes, and dahlias. I buy dill plants from the nursery, but the herb can be directly grown from seed in the beds after the last chance of frost. You can also extend the harvest by sowing seeds every couple of weeks through the warm summer months.

FEVERFEW

Although feverfew (*Tanacetum parthenium*) is considered a medicinal herb (the name derives from the Latin *febrifugia*, or "fever reducer"), I grow it primarily for arrangements. This member of the daisy family features flowers with a similar

This bunch of flowering dill in a white earthenware vase serves as a reminder that an abundance of one flower in a plain vessel can speak volumes.

'Strawberry Blonde' calendula
Common lavender
Common chives

'Magic Single' feverfew
'Bouquet' dill
Lemon verbena

Sage
'Aurea' elderflower
Borage

profile: white petals surrounding bright yellow centers. Feverfew flower heads are much smaller than daisies, however, with short, overlapping petals and flat centers. Feverfew reseeds itself in the raised beds, yet I can't resist sowing a fresh crop each spring, for security's sake. The sprigs provide a bright, airy note to bouquets of all kinds.

Feverfew flowers also make a lovely tea with a tangy scent reminiscent of freshly mown grass. When used as a natural dye, the tea produces a pale yellow color.

SAGE

Among the flowers in the raised beds in my tennis court garden, a large bush of sage (*Salvia officinalis*) returns triumphantly each year. I trim back the branch tops in early spring, when the bush starts to revive itself from its winter sleep, but otherwise this fast-growing garden stalwart is largely self-sufficient. Its vibrant purple flowers bloom around early June through July and are a favorite with both the native bees and honeybees. I also cut branches, especially when it is blooming, for flower arrangements. Because I find the scent calming, I like to rub the leaves when I am walking around the raised beds. After the plant finishes blooming, I leave the blossoms to dry, as they are still visited by the pollinators in the garden.

LAVENDER

Just outside the greenhouse there's a nice clump of lavender (genus *Lavandula*) that seems quite happy. The spot is warmed by full sun during the day and the heater vent that juts outside the greenhouse wall above it. As long as I trim the lavender back thoroughly in spring, the bush provides plenty of sprigs to use for cooking and to fill my vases. I find that lavender tends to get lost in larger arrangements, so I display it all by itself, often by the potting wheel in my studio so that I can smell its wonderful perfume while I work.

To augment the few lavender plants I have, I buy the herb in pots in spring and plant them around the raised beds. There are many wonderful types, with differently shaped blooms, and my local nursery (Gilbertie's) offers a couple dozen varieties. My lavender favorites are *Lavandula angustifolia* 'Munstead' and 'Hidcote' and × *intermedia* 'Provence'. Each has a distinct flower head and shade of purple with slightly different blooming times.

I use fresh lavender to make ice cream sweetened with honey or rub it into granulated sugar to flavor a cake batter. I don't usually have enough of a harvest to dry the lavender, though the plants are readily available for purchase at Gilbertie's if I decide I want more.

BORAGE

Borage is one of the essential flowering herbs for my arrangements and a great favorite of the bees and butterflies. I prefer the classic blue borage flowers (*Borago officinalis*) to the white variety (*B. officinalis* 'Alba'), as I have lots of white flowers in the garden and prize blue for its rarity. The flowers bloom at the same time as the early lilies, poppies, verbascums, and roses, and the bright blue is a fantastic foil to reds, yellows, and sherbet colors. Sometimes the borage plants reseed, but I order fresh ones for spring, as I can't rely on the plant returning. I place them inside and outside of the garden fences in sunny areas because borage is not attractive to deer or other animals. The stiff, hairy stems are benign but can irritate the skin when you are cutting them from the plant. These stems are great for supporting other flowers in a vase, and borage flowers hold up well in arrangements, too. I especially like to use the edible flowers in salads (they pair well with beets) and as a garnish for cakes.

VERBENA

I grow lemon verbena (*Aloysia citrodora*) and *Verbena bonariensis* in the raised beds. Though they have similarities—both are part of the vervain family and are native to Chile and Argentina—they have very different functions in the garden.

Lemon verbena is an annual herb with bright green foliage, a spray of pale pink to white flowers, and a fantastic lemony fragrance that perfumes any room. I use the strong branches and fragrant leaves as a basis for an arrangement because they hold up other flowers so well. In springtime, I buy fresh plants and then harvest and dry the leaves in fall before the first frost, storing them in paper bags for use as tea throughout the winter months.

Verbena bonariensis, sometimes called tall verbena or Brazilian vervain, is a perennial plant; its tall stems hold themselves upright even in the wind and rain, and the clusters of purple flowers at the top provide nice accents in arrangements. *V. bonariensis* is not particular about soil and will grow (and reseed) just about anywhere there's full sun. I toss out the seed in spring and wait to see where it will decide to sprout. It particularly likes to make its home in the cracks in the old tennis court and the middle of the raised beds, between the dahlia plants, where it is a magnet for butterflies, bees, and most other insects.

CHIVE FLOWER

I grow two types of chives in my garden: the common variety (*Allium schoenoprasum*), which has pungent purple flowers that are perfect to use in cooking, and the slightly taller, white-flowered garlic chives (*A. tuberosum*). I use the former with a standby fish-in-parchment recipe (see page 152) that makes great use of the chive flowers at the height

When flowering herbs are at their peak of freshness and flavor, I put a mixed bouquet of them in a vase in the kitchen. Marigold, borage, dill, and allium petals are perfect to toss into salads, and sage is essential for roast chicken.

of their bloom time. I am not sure how the garlic chives arrived in the garden, but they have seeded pervasively at the bases of the raised beds. I leave them alone because they are such a favorite of the bees. I cut the common chives after the heads have turned grayish in color and have dried, which allows the plant (hopefully) a second chance to bloom in the cooler fall months. Both types like full sun and are not fussy about soil or location. Once established, this perennial herb will return faithfully. I fertilize the clumps with the organic fish emulsion that I spray over the entire garden every two weeks or so throughout the hot summer months.

ELDERFLOWER

The wild native bushes of elderflower that line our road and neighborhood in June and July give off a strong, sweet fragrance. A couple of years ago, I bought two types of elderflower (*Sambucus canadensis* 'Nova' and 'Aurea') as small, 1-foot (30.5 cm) rooted plants in pots and planted them near the hydrangeas in our yard, where they get the full sun they prefer. The bushes have now grown to full height (as tall as 8 feet/2.4 m) and produce the fragrant flowers that I use in my arrangements. (I also use elderflower in the kitchen to make syrup.) Once the unpicked flowers turn into berries, I leave them on the tree for the birds.

CALENDULA

Calendula officinalis is also known as pot marigold, but it belongs to a different genus from the more commonly known garden marigolds (with calendula native to Africa and Europe and marigolds to southwestern North America and South America). It is a member of the daisy family, which can be confusing, but I focus on the flower shape, color, and time of bloom and don't worry about the nomenclature.

Calendula can be grown from seed in small pots or directly sown into the garden. In late April, I purchase the plants at a local nursery, where they are sold with other annual herbs. They like good organic soil and full sun. I've found calendula is happiest in the cooler seasons yet even holds its own during the hot and humid August weather here in Connecticut. The plants perk up in September, and I have often observed them still blooming after a frost.

The calendula flower head has beautiful small petals that radiate from the center. It is one of my favorite flowers to press into plaster (see page 176), as the shape is expressive when formed in clay. As a bonus, the bright orange petals, when separated from the stem and head, taste delicious in salads.

Borage, feverfew, foxglove, clematis, nigella, and verbascum have a summery and airy feel when placed together in a porcelain pitcher. The effect is of an armload of flowers that doesn't necessarily feel "arranged"—in a good way.

HALIBUT WITH CHIVES IN PARCHMENT

My copy of Alice Waters's *Chez Panisse Menu Cookbook* from the 1980s is worn and falling apart. Over the years, I have made many variations of her fish en papillote recipe. I especially love cooking fish in parchment when the chive flowers are abundant in the raised beds; I use them to make a compound butter and to garnish each serving. The dish can be assembled on the baking sheet a few hours ahead of serving and put in the refrigerator, which is great for a dinner party when you don't want to be doing everything last-minute. The fish (still on the sheet) should be brought to room temperature before cooking. I use halibut here, but the recipe is so adaptable that any firm-fleshed fish will work; you can also swap out the vegetables, depending on the season. Serve the fish and vegetables with rice or another grain. *Serves 4*

3 tablespoons olive oil, plus more for brushing the parchment

3 medium leeks, sliced into thin rounds and well washed to remove any grit

4 ounces (115 g) shiitake mushrooms, stems removed and caps thinly sliced

Coarse salt and freshly ground black pepper

¼ cup (60 ml) heavy cream

2 large lemons, finely zested (to equal 2 tablespoons) and then halved

½ cup (15 g) chive flowers, coarsely chopped, plus more for garnish

4 tablespoons (60 g) butter, softened

½ cup (15 g) chopped chive greens

½ cup (15 g) chopped parsley

1½ pounds (455 g) halibut (or Scottish or coho salmon), divided into 4 pieces

A few fresh thyme sprigs

Cut four sheets of parchment paper, each about 9 by 12 inches (23 by 30 cm) long. Preheat the oven to 450°F (230°C).

In a cast-iron skillet, heat the oil over medium heat; add the leeks, mushrooms, and salt and pepper to taste, and gently sauté the leeks and mushrooms until soft, 3 to 5 minutes. Add the cream, 1 tablespoon of the lemon zest, and the juice of ½ lemon. Cook until the vegetables have absorbed the cream, then remove the skillet from the heat and fold in half of the chopped chive flowers.

In a small bowl, mash the softened butter. Add the chive greens, the remaining lemon zest, most of the parsley (reserve a tablespoon or two for garnish), and the juice of ¼ lemon. Season with salt and pepper, then divide the butter mixture into 4 pieces.

Working with 1 piece of parchment at a time, arrange the parchment so that the fish will be placed on the center of one half of the shorter side. Brush this area lightly with oil.

Place one-quarter of the mushroom mixture on this oiled area, then top with a piece of fish. Season the fish with salt and pepper, then top with a portion of the compound butter. Repeat with the remaining parchment, mushroom mixture, fish, and compound butter, then squeeze the remaining 2 lemon halves over all 4 pieces of fish. Top with the thyme sprigs and the remaining chopped chive flowers.

Fold each piece of parchment loosely over the top of the fish and roll and crimp the edges tightly to seal. Place the packets on a baking sheet. Bake for 8 to 12 minutes, depending on the thickness of the fish and how well done you like it.

Carefully open each packet (watch out for steam). Sprinkle with a few additional chive flowers and serve.

PART IV

SEROTINAL

MID-AUGUST TO MID-SEPTEMBER ARE GENERALLY
the hottest days of the year, known as the serotinal period (*sero*
means "late" in Latin). In the garden, much of the plant life is
rich in saturated color. Picture a field of sunflowers in bloom,
or a bunch of zinnias and marigolds held together in a glass jar.
Everywhere you look, there are leaves of the most spectacular
shapes and sizes, the kind you want to include in arrangements
for the distinct character they bring. Many of the flowers have
sturdier stems than those that blossomed just a few weeks or
months earlier, and they last longer in a vase, despite the heat.
(The heavy stalks of gladioli and sunflowers are two such
examples.)

This is the time when we head toward the crescendo of
the long growing season. The blazing heat can cause seeds to
be released. Around the same time as the daylight hours grow
shorter, I take care to deadhead any plant that requires it and
stake stems that have grown too tall and are falling over.

Hydrangeas

There are four *Hydrangea paniculata* trees with white flower heads on the side of our house that predate our arrival. They appear to be very old, and they flower majestically late in summer every year.

Within the genus *Hydrangea* are about seventy distinct species of hydrangeas. Some are native to North America (fossils have been found in the United States that date back forty to sixty-five million years), and other species were planted in China during the Ming dynasty (1366–1644) as well as in eighth-century Japan. The plants were brought to Europe by Americans in the first half of the eighteenth century.

The name *hydrangea* comes from the Greek words *hydros*, meaning "water," and *angos*, meaning "jar," because the plant requires steady watering to keep it from drooping. Hydrangeas prefer full sun (with perhaps some shade in the afternoon sun) and good, healthy soil. There are many opinions about whether to trim the flower heads from the shrubs after blooming, in early spring, or in fall. My strategy is to take the path of least resistance: I cut the stems and flowers for arrangements but otherwise leave the shrubs alone, and they all bloom well the following year. (Even as I write this, in February, there are dried flower heads atop the long, leafless branches that provide seeds and habitat for birds and insects over the long winter.)

On a visit to an estate in the French countryside, I saw the most extravagant long row of blue hydrangea bushes, which made me think of the playing-card gardeners in *Alice's Adventures in Wonderland* who painted the white rosebushes red to please the Queen. The hydrangeas were not native to the Provençal soil, so the gardeners on the estate must have had to go through all sorts of machinations to adjust the soil pH for a higher acid content to keep the hydrangeas blooming blue. Years later, I planted one petite blue Endless Summer *Hydrangea macrophylla* against a stone wall by the house, and it is a challenge to keep deer and squirrels from eating the tempting flowers. But because it is such a wonderful blue, I persevere. In addition, I planted an Incrediball hydrangea next to the greenhouse and a few oakleaf hydrangeas (*H. quercifolia*) at the back of my gas kiln building. Together with the very old white hydrangeas I inherited when we moved in, these shrubs and trees provide flower heads in a nice variety of shapes for my bouquets. I like to arrange them by themselves or, on occasion, in a wild grouping of everything that's in bloom at once.

An earthenware vase filled with hydrangeas, Japanese anemones, and dahlias is embellished with clay flowers molded from those in my garden. I first cast the flowers in plaster and then press clay into the mold; once dry, the appliqués are pressed onto a clay pot before glazing and firing.

Gladioli

Gladioli certainly lack subtlety. I love their exquisite form, as well as their surprisingly wide range of colors, from cool, creamy whites and pale pastels to the brightest shades of red, hot fuchsia, lime green, and beyond. Even the white ones seem to glow audaciously from within.

I had been familiar with the flowering stalks for many years, but it wasn't until I traveled to Denmark about a decade ago that I had my first true appreciation of gladioli. Seeing row upon row of them growing at a pick-your-own farm, I was entranced by the unevenness of the flowers, in all stages of bloom. There was no order to the arrangement of colors in each row, and the glads were planted alongside rows of dahlias and sunflowers, to magical, joyful effect.

From there, we traveled to the museum at nearby Egeskov Castle; the garden there was full of gladioli, which were interspersed with dahlias, carnations, zinnias, sweet peas, calendulas, and other summer beauties. The August weather in Denmark allowed for all sorts of flowers to bloom at once, and the spectacle filled me with new ideas for planting gladioli. Returning home, I researched the best places from which to order these magnificent flowers, my favorite being Honker Flats (see page 280).

Gladioli are native to Africa and the Mediterranean. During the eighteenth century, species of gladiolus were introduced to Northern Europe. In the early 1800s in England, four or five different species were hybridized to develop the modern types we grow today.

The name *gladiolus* originates from the Latin word *gladius*, or "sword of the gladiator," no doubt from the long, spear-like shape of the flowers. Over the years, they have come to symbolize strength of character, sincerity, and moral integrity. For this reason, they are traditionally included in arrangements for funerals, to honor the deceased. Consequently, they were grown commercially on a large scale to supply flowers for funeral homes; along the way, they seemed to have lost much of their personality.

In the last few years, however, gladioli have started to come back into fashion, especially less common varieties of the flower grown on small farms and by home gardeners. These examples boast multiple, beautifully formed flower heads and a more distinctive, organic feel than the familiar gladioli found in wholesale and retail markets.

HOW TO GROW GLADIOLI

Gladioli flower ten to twelve weeks after planting, and the sowing can be staggered every two weeks over the summer months to get a continual bloom. All

Freshly cut stalks of gladioli laid in a row on the tennis court surface illustrate just how lush and saturated their colors can be. The 'Peter Pears', 'Plum Tart', and 'Trader Horn' varieties—along with one deep red zinnia—will next be combined in a tall vase.

gladioli are extremely easy to plant; the corms are not large and are generally planted 2 to 4 inches (5 to 10 cm) below the soil surface and a few inches (8 cm) apart from each other in the beds. They go into the soil in my raised beds at the same time as the dahlia tubers—that is, once the danger of frost has passed (around mid–May). I weave them in and out among the roses, bearded irises, dahlias, and marigolds.

Glad corms can be dug up in fall, stored, and replanted in the garden in spring, in a process very similar to that of dahlia tubers (see page 200). Truthfully though, I usually leave mine in the ground and purchase new corms every spring. Sometimes the previous year's corms will survive the winter cold and sprout sooner than the newly planted ones, but I don't rely on this.

Their forms are easy to recognize, with leaves that slightly resemble those of an iris but are more slender and delicate. To prevent the long stalks from falling over and bending, tie the stems to a stake when they reach their full height but before their flowers open. Admittedly, I enjoy when the stems become a little wonky (due to my reluctance to stake them); there's something quite pleasing about watching the stems bend (but not break) in a serpentine fashion, like the ones that so enchanted me years ago in Denmark.

HOW TO ARRANGE GLADIOLI

For arranging, a tall, narrow, sturdy vase is best to support gladioli. Tulipieres are perfect for displaying the tall stalks, as the stems fit in the different openings so nicely. Once the flowers appear, you can pull off spent blooms at the top, without worrying that those below won't open. You can also continue to cut the end of each stem, which allows fresh access to the water in the vase and keeps them from drying out.

In mixed arrangements, I pair gladioli with the other cheery annuals such as zinnias, cosmos, calendulas, and dahlias for a vibrant, hot palette.

Gladioli and lilies provide the staccato notes to a foundational arrangement of zinnias, roses, sweet peas, and larkspurs. The shorter-cut stems support the taller ones and keep them from falling over.

FAVORITE VARIETIES

Gladiolus callianthus An heirloom glad from 1888 with white flowers and a strong fragrance

G. 'Black Star' The darkest, wine-red color with small white brushstrokes down the center of each petal

G. 'Chocolate' Gorgeous cocoa- and lavender-colored flowers

G. 'Dauntless' An heirloom glad from 1940 colored in deep pink with a splash of scarlet in the throat

G. 'Mon Amour' A 3-foot (1 m) stalk with bicolor (mauve and pale yellow) flowers

G. 'Peter Pears' A glorious apricot with huge blooms

G. 'Plum Tart' Stalks that grow more than 3 feet (1 m) high, with flowers in a stunning magenta color

G. 'Trader Horn' Scarlet blooms with white centers that add great cheer to any mixed arrangement

THE CAMARADERIE OF FLOWER GROWERS

Many of my most passionate pursuits—gardening, pottery, taking still life photographs—are largely solitary exercises. I enjoy being in the studio and the garden by myself, often in silence, which allows me the space to think clearly and work out ideas.

Nevertheless, I make sure to carve out plenty of time to spend with other gardeners. It's heavenly to sit with a group of like-minded friends and talk about plants, the weather, and the tasks at hand on our respective to-do lists. The community of flower growers, arrangers, and enthusiasts greatly enhances my life and work. Over the last few decades, I've found that "flower people," as I call them, are among the most optimistic souls, with an admirable perspective about the state of the world and a determination to move things forward in a positive direction.

Since I started growing flowers for my work, I've made it a habit to attend garden symposia to hear speakers discuss all sorts of issues, including biodiversity, invasive plants, caring for and pruning trees, soil development, garden design, and the slow flower movement.

It's not only fun to have so many people in the same place at one time to talk to, it's also inspirational and informative. We discuss our common concerns, troubleshoot and trade solutions, and share sources and plants. (The 'Leda' roses pictured opposite were a gift from my garden friends Page Dickey and Bosco Schell. I think of the two of them every time the roses bloom.) When I get home from these engagements, I consider how I can apply all the things I've just learned to my own garden efforts.

Several times a year, I enjoy giving talks to garden clubs and love to hear feedback about all aspects of my work—the flowers, the pots, and the photographs. The audience questions provide valuable insight. One of the things I am told is that my pieces make flower arranging very easy, because the shapes naturally hold flowers well. This is a goal that I aim for. Being a part of this garden universe inspires new pots for new flowers.

There is a society for just about every botanical interest, and a simple search online will find a nearby chapter. I flow in and out of memberships but am a constant participant in the American Dahlia Society as well as the Aspetuck Land Trust, which is only a mile (1.6 km) from my home. In addition to being an active member of the Garden Conservancy, which is a national organization, I like to support local gardens, as these are so important to the community, and I recommend finding like-minded groups in your own region.

Sunflowers

There is nothing more joyful than seeing a sunflower with birds and bees perching on the leaves and flower heads reaching toward the sky. I consider it a harbinger of high summer and an essential flower in the cutting garden, not least because sunflowers are quite easy to grow. They generally bloom alongside summer annuals including marigolds, zinnias, and salvias.

Native to the Americas, where they have grown for thousands of years, sunflowers belong to the genus *Helianthus*. The seeds made their way to Europe in the seventeenth century. The flowers are still cultivated today in great numbers in countries that produce cooking oil and seeds for consumption. In France, I have marveled at the sight of vast fields of sunflowers growing in the summer sun.

My favorite aspect of the sunflower is the staggered arrangement of its center circle of seeds in a true Fibonacci sequence. The mathematical formula is named for Leonardo Pisano Fibonacci, a medieval Italian mathematician who, in 1202, wrote about how these numbers in sequence create the perfect spiral pattern found in nature: 0, 1, 1, 2, 3, 5, 8, 13, 21, 34, 55, 89, 144 . . . This corresponds to the composition of seeds on the head of a sunflower, so that the position of each one is rotated a bit on its side for maximum exposure to sunlight. In the morning, the sunflower faces the east, and it rotates its head to follow the sun across the day. I often go out into the garden at various times to observe where the sunflower head has turned. Sunflowers are not the only blossoms that feature this mathematical sequence in their centers and petals, but to me, they are the most dramatic example of nature's brilliance.

HOW TO GROW SUNFLOWERS

I grow two types of sunflowers: one to sustain wildlife in my garden and one exclusively for cutting. First, I plant the mammoth variety, *Helianthus annuus*, which can grow up to 16 feet (5 m) tall. I order the 'Mammoth Russian' or 'Mammoth Grey Stripe' for the enormous flower heads, which provide bounty for the birds, bees, and squirrels; nearly every seed company has its own giant sunflower seed version. The seeds can be directly sown a couple of inches (5 cm) deep into the garden bed once the soil has warmed, which usually means mid-May here in Connecticut. To ensure successive blooming, I plant new seeds for the next couple of weeks. The back of the seed packet should say how many weeks are required for maturity. Sometimes more seeds are in order when the snails, birds, and squirrels eat the emerging plants, so I watch closely and

'Sonja', ProCut 'Orange', and 'Moulin Rouge' sunflowers are held in place by a flower frog in a footed bowl, then surrounded with coral Benary's Giant zinnias, calendula, and rudbeckia. Grapes and their leaves, snipped from the tennis court fence, are added at the end for a trailing effect.

Below: One morning I noticed a bunch of empty sunflower shells deposited on a large sunflower head. The birds must have stood there, leaned over to remove the seeds from the underside, eaten their share, and left the remnants behind.

Opposite: 'Lemon Queen' sunflowers grow wonderfully high in the round garden.

sow again if the first round disappears from the garden bed. This year, I will use the snail guard that I discovered last summer in a biodynamic garden (see page 100).

I place the mammoth seeds in the middle of the raised beds, to accommodate the massive height of the sunflowers and allow any shorter plants around them to access the sun. (With tall plants, it's important to note and account for the shade they will cast as they continue to grow.) Once the stalks have reached their full height, I strip the large lower leaves, otherwise they will stunt the growth of the nearby dahlias.

These giants need staking. As their heads get heavy, they bow over easily; one strong windstorm can knock them over completely. In fall, once the centers have been picked clean of seeds by the birds, I leave the stalks and empty heads like skeletons in the garden, where they stand quietly through the winter months.

The second sunflower type I grow includes varieties bred for cutting, such as the ProCut Series, which produce multiple branches and flower heads and thus greatly increase the possibilities for my arrangements. This type of sunflower also requires successive planting to provide the longest availability.

HOW TO ARRANGE SUNFLOWERS

Branching sunflowers can give structure and support to other flowers in a bouquet. I leave the branches longer, cut away the lower leaves, and anchor the stalks in a flower frog at the bottom of a bowl or in a vase. Or, when arranging sunflowers by themselves, I cut the stalks short and place them in one big mass in a container. Freshly cut sunflowers can last four to five days in a vase. I rarely change the water. Once the petals start to fade, I disassemble the arrangement and toss the flowers into the compost.

I DO MY BEST THINKING IN THE GARDEN

It's no secret that I am happiest when I am busy, and each day finds me trying to be as productive as possible, with various projects at different stages of development in the studio. When I travel, I'm not one for beach vacations, preferring to spend time walking around cities or taking in every detail of a museum or garden. In my own garden, however, I stand or sit and listen to the birds and insects, watch the bees as they make their way in and out of the boxes, and observe flowers moving when a breeze happens to blow. In these moments, the most active thing I do is clip or tie up a stem in the raised beds. For the most part, I try to just be, with no immediate task at hand or to-do list in mind.

Often I'll hold still and listen intently for the vibration of hummingbird wings or lean in close to admire the smallest bloom or take in the drama of an enormous flower head. As the herbalist Rosemary Gladstar said, "Talking to the plants is one way of talking directly to the spirit." The flowers exist just as they are; they don't take world events into account, but just blossom in their own fashion.

Even when the weather is lousy, I make sure to get outside and mosey around with no agenda in mind. The rain colors the garden in a way that invites ruminating among the raised beds when everything is wet. When I was a child and there was a downpour, I would use my mother's opera glasses as binoculars and head to the yard with our family dog to study the apple trees. I often think of this and am amazed at how long ago that was. There is a sense of time passing as the seasons come and go, and an acknowledgment that each moment is meant to be savored.

When the news is stressful or a work problem feels overwhelming, I'll head to the garden with a cup of tea and sit on a bench away from the bees. I breathe deeply to calm down and put things back into perspective before returning to my own hive of activity: the studio with its pottery wheels.

The daily time in the garden often leads to a creative breakthrough, even when I'm performing routine tasks. Among the plants, my actions may be rote, but it's the repetitive motions that set me to pondering. In my head, I see the relationships with flowers that are about to bloom and the vases in my studio. I focus on the luminosity and colors coming through the leaves and petals, and the way that a passionflower vine wraps around a stake, for example. I like to move along the beds and pull out plants (I hesitate to call them weeds) that are crowding out others and keep things in check. I'll stake flowers and deadhead where needed. All the while I can address any problems I may be having and hopefully come up with a solution that renews my spirit.

Echinaceas and Rudbeckias

Years ago, I planted echinacea along with rudbeckia in the round garden because I loved the odd color combination of the yellow and fuchsia flowers. Just past the midway point of summer, these two perennial flowers begin to appear, bringing with them a profusion of color and character.

Both plants are easy to grow and maintain even for fledgling gardeners. They are known as coneflowers (and members of the aster family) and are native to North America, where they were used by Indigenous peoples to treat snakebites, sore throats, and coughs, but they are not the same flower. You can see the differences in their centers—rudbeckias tend to have flat dark brown or black centers, which is why they also are often called black- or brown-eyed Susans, whereas echinaceas have a spiky central cone that is orange, brown, or green. Rudbeckia petals are on the same flat plane as the center; echinacea petals droop from the center. Both types of coneflower are used in meadows, raised beds, and cutting gardens and are very attractive to bees and butterflies as pollinators.

ECHINACEA

If you have ever run your hand across the center of an echinacea flower, you will understand how the name was conceived. The word *echinacea* was coined by the German botanist Conrad Moench, who revised Swedish botanist Carl Linnaeus's classification of this plant as *Rudbeckia purpurea*. Moench created a new name from the Greek *echinos*, meaning "hedgehog" or "sea urchin" (a reference to the flower's texture), and the Latin *āceus*, for the prickly nature of the disk florets.

I was drawn to echinacea because of the deep pink color of its petals that surround an orange center. The plants can be started as seeds or found at plant nurseries in spring. They like full sun

Below: I love how the orange cones and fuchsia petals of this echinacea align visually with the tiger lilies growing alongside them.

Opposite: I photographed this arrangement of echinacea, nigella, and white scabiosa against a moody black background. The shadows bring out the beautiful nuance of the orange cones and petals.

and just about any soil; they are drought resistant. Around thirty-five coneflower hybrids make up this family of plants, but I stick with the classic *Echinacea purpurea* and look forward to seeing it in the garden for summer bouquets. The only issue I have in growing echinacea is keeping the deer from eating it. I assumed that native plants were not attractive to the animals. Turns out I was wrong, but I have found that using an organic deer repellent (such as Plantskydd) is effective.

RUDBECKIA

I was first drawn to rudbeckia because I liked that its hues were similar to those of the sunflower, only with smaller flower heads. I was looking for a plant at that scale to combine with both dahlias and sunflowers, which bloom around the same time (late summer and early autumn). I have grown numerous types of rudbeckia, but their common thread is an eternal cheerfulness.

Comprising twenty-five species, rudbeckia plants were brought from North America to Europe by Spanish explorers and subsequently made their way across the continent. In 1753, Linnaeus named the flowers after his teacher Olof Rudbeck.

Rudbeckias like full sun, can handle dry periods during summer, and are deer resistant. All types are available in seed form; I directly sow them after the chance of frost is past. I also order a

Opposite: A boisterous celebration of the season in an ash-glazed, wood-fired vase includes *Rudbeckia triloba* and *R. hirta* 'Cherokee Sunset Mix' and 'Autumn Sunset', white and pink echinacea, *Cosmos sulphureus*, and bee balm.

Left: 'Henry Eilers' rudbeckia blooms for several weeks in both the tennis court and round gardens.

variety of plugs from my local nursery every spring, because I have found that the squirrels, birds, and voles often eat the seedlings, making survival to the point of full bloom somewhat fraught.

FAVORITE RUDBECKIA VARIETIES

Rudbeckia hirta Daisylike in appearance but with bright yellow petals and deep brown centers

R. hirta 'Cherokee Sunset Mix' Coneflower seeds in a beautiful range of autumnal shades—bronze and copper oranges, reds, and yellows

R. subtomentosa 'Henry Eilers' Unusual coneflowers often compared to asterisks, thanks to thin, distinctly quilled, bright yellow petals emanating from dark brown centers

R. triloba Commonly known as brown-eyed Susan, with smaller flowers, dark, hairy stems, rough leaves, and a longer bloom window than its black-eyed cousin

The dramatic brown and gold 'Cherokee Sunset Mix' rudbeckia grows abundantly on the tennis court. The markings are mirrored in the petals of the 'Autumn Beauty' sunflower in this ruffle-edged earthenware vase.

Cosmos

If ever a flower could be described as having a sweet disposition and easy demeanor, it's the cosmos. With wonderfully airy stems and wispy flower heads, cosmos appear to wave in the wind as they come into bloom, which is around the same time as zinnias and marigolds. I consider them an indispensable presence in the cutting garden, where they hold up quite well alongside the dahlias, and often last until the first frost.

I plant cosmos around the edges of the raised beds, so that they can billow out as they grow. I have had some cosmos plants reach as tall as 5 feet (1.5 m). They also self-seed in the cracks in the pavement on the old tennis court. In the round garden, I situate them so that they fill in around the old roses just as those bushes are done blooming. To produce new growth and blooms, you need to consistently deadhead. Take care not to overwater the plants, or they will lose their vigor.

The name *cosmos* comes from the Greek word for "world," which makes sense given the way their petals are so neatly ordered in a circle around the center and seem to be a universe unto themselves. Cosmos flowers are easy to start from seed, but recently I've been buying cosmos as plugs from farms (especially for the more pastel varieties).

Chocolate cosmos are sold as bare roots, which I start in pots in the greenhouse in early April, planting them in the garden in May. (They really smell like chocolate!)

Every autumn, I make plaster casts of fresh garden flowers, and cosmos are always front and center in this exercise. Their flower heads lend themselves particularly well to a clear imprint. I gather blossoms and place them into a box of liquid plaster to capture the shapes, which I then mold with clay to use on some of my pots (see page 157 for an example of a vase made with this technique).

A blue-and-white slip pitcher holds brilliantly colored 'Bright Lights' and 'Dazzler' cosmos along with 'Giant Orange' marigolds and goldenrod, all of which last a long time once cut and placed in a vase.

FAVORITE VARIETIES

Cosmos atrosanguineus Chocolate cosmos, dramatic and arresting, with the distinct scent of cocoa powder

C. bipinnatus 'Bright Lights' A brilliant orange variety that's bright and cheerful

C. bipinnatus Cupcakes Series A favorite for its fringed, delicate, papery pastel petals

C. bipinnatus 'Sea Shells' Brightly colored, especially charming blooms named for the petal shape, which resembles seashells

C. bipinnatus 'Sensation Picotee' Among the prettiest and most arresting cosmos, with large white flowers edged in a deep rosy pink

C. bipinnatus Sonata Series Charming, small daisylike flowers in a multitude of colors (white, pink, red, purple, and burgundy)

C. bipinnatus 'Versailles Tetra' A deep pink and fuchsia single petal designed for early blooming

Marigolds

The English name *marigold* is a reference to the Virgin Mary, but the flowers are native to Mexico and were used by the Aztec people (who called them cempasúchil) for religious and medicinal purposes. They symbolize the brevity of life and are used to celebrate El Día de los Muertos, or the Day of the Dead, on November 1. From Mexico, they made their way to Spain and then spread to France and parts of Africa, where the taller varieties were bred. Spanish and Portuguese sailors transported marigold seeds to India more than 350 years ago. In that time, the flowers became an important presence in many Indian celebrations, including Diwali, as well as in weddings and religious festivals.

When I first built raised beds on the tennis court in 2012, I planned to grow vegetables, especially a wide variety of heirloom tomatoes, as the surface of the court was warm and in full sun. I started cultivating marigolds as companion plants to tomatoes because their flowers attract bees and other insects that are beneficial to the tomato plants while deterring deer and rodents with their strong scent. I've since found growing tomatoes a tricky business, so I decided to dedicate the raised beds to flowers. Ever since, I have planted marigolds in a range of sizes and colors in the cracks of the asphalt tennis court; I find it amusing

to see them there in late summer and fall, especially the giant yellow-and-orange ones that grow to about 3 feet (1 m) high.

Though marigolds can be directly sown into the garden or in pots, I mostly buy mine as small plugs at local nurseries and plant them in mid–May, after I have put in the dahlia tubers.

Once cut, marigolds last well in a vase. Their scent is strong and earthy. The thick stems create an excellent support system in arrangements. Marigolds go in a vase wonderfully with sunflowers, gladioli, zinnias, cosmos, and hydrangeas that are blooming at the same moment. Beyond cutting and arranging the flowers, I use the marigold heads as a natural dye for linen napkins (see page 183) and in some recipes, like the risotto on page 180.

For this voluminous arrangement of marigolds, dahlias, helianthus, zinnias, and goldenrod, I chose a footed terra-cotta urn because the warm tones of the clay mirror those of the flowers.

FAVORITE VARIETIES

Tagetes erecta **'Giant Orange' and 'Giant Yellow'** Strong-scented, large flower heads of orange or yellow, on 3-foot-tall (1 m) stems

T. patula **Durango Series** Yellow-and-orange and yellow-striped flower heads that pair well in short bouquets with zinnias and cosmos

T. patula **'Queen Sophia'** A beautifully patterned marigold with petals that are deep orange with a beautiful yellow outline

T. tenuifolia **'Tangerine Gem'** A tiny variety (only 10 to 12 inches/ 25 to 30 cm high) with orange flowers that are delicious in salads

RISOTTO WITH FRESH FLOWERS

Risotto is a great comfort food any time of the year. I often make it for dinner and incorporate the most delicious vegetables of the season, usually purchased from the organic farm just down the road. When the marigolds (or calendulas) are in the garden, they make a beautiful and fragrant last hurrah to the bowl and help all the flavors meld. I love the rich yellow color of the petals, which accent the zucchini and bell peppers in this version. *Serves 4 to 6*

4 tablespoons (60 ml) extra virgin olive oil
1 red bell pepper, cored, seeded, and
  coarsely chopped
1 fennel bulb, coarsely chopped
1 zucchini, coarsely chopped
1 garlic clove, finely chopped
Coarse salt and freshly ground black
  pepper
½ lemon
4 tablespoons (60 g) unsalted butter
1 onion, finely chopped

1 cup (220 g) Arborio or carnaroli rice
¾ cup (180 ml) dry white wine
1 quart (950 ml) vegetable stock
1 cup (65 g) chopped fresh cilantro leaves,
  loosely packed
Finely grated Parmesan cheese, for garnish
  (optional)
A handful of fresh marigold or calendula
  flowers, or a combination of the two,
  flower heads separated into petals

In a skillet, heat the olive oil over medium heat. Add the bell pepper, fennel, zucchini, and garlic and season with salt and black pepper. Cook, stirring occasionally, until the vegetables are tender, 5 to 7 minutes. Squeeze the lemon half over the vegetables and turn off the heat.

In a Dutch oven, melt 2 tablespoons of the butter over low heat. Add the onion and sauté until translucent, 3 to 5 minutes (you do not want the onion to brown). Stir in the rice and toss to coat in the butter-onion mixture. Season with salt and black pepper.

Increase the heat to medium and stir in the wine. Cook, stirring, until the liquid is reduced by half, about 3 minutes. Gradually add the stock to the pot, about ½ cup (120 ml) at a time, continuing to stir and waiting until the liquid is mostly absorbed by the rice before adding more. Cook until the rice is soft but al dente, retaining a bit of firmness, 15 to 20 minutes total.

Stir in the cooked vegetables and the remaining 2 tablespoons butter. Season with salt and black pepper and stir in the cilantro.

Divide the risotto among serving bowls and top each with Parmesan, if desired. Scatter flower petals over each serving.

MAKING MARIGOLD-DYED NAPKINS

Lately, as a way to make good use of all the beautiful garden bounty, I've been delving into ideas for utilizing the flowers beyond arrangements. Natural dyes for textiles seemed like an obvious choice, and I am just beginning to discover how to make and use them, enjoying the trial and error. Napkins are a manageable size and easy enough to find (or to make yourself, with even minimal sewing skills), and marigolds capture the most gorgeous yellow, which transfers nicely to fabrics. I also like to include goldenrod and calendula in the mix, depending on what's in bloom in the garden.

Note: Before you begin, keep in mind that this process unfolds over several days and requires a digital scale and a hot plate. You'll get best results from 100 percent linen or cotton fabrics; I have tested the dyeing with both and have been equally happy with the outcome.

Tools & Materials

8 linen or cotton napkins (I used dinner-sized ones, 18 to 20 inches/46 to 51 cm square)

2 large (about 12-quart/11 L) stockpots

Mild dishwashing detergent (such as Dawn)

Face mask

Apron

Rubber gloves

Alum (for mordanting the napkins; the amount will depend on the weight of your fabric)

Candy thermometer or other instant-read thermometer

Metal tongs

Fresh and/or dried marigolds, goldenrod, or calendula (or a combination; the amount will depend on the weight of your fabric)

Prepare the napkins for dyeing: Weigh the napkins on a digital scale. (Mine weighed 370 grams total.) Jot this number down; you will refer to it twice.

Fill one of the stockpots with water and stir in 1 tablespoon of the dishwashing detergent. Add the napkins, stirring to submerge, and soak overnight. This should help remove the sizing from commercially produced napkins, which is used in the manufacturing process to improve its strength and prolong its wear.

The next day, rinse the napkins in cold water until any soap bubbles disappear. Rinse and dry the stockpot.

Put a kettle of water on to boil. Wearing a face mask, apron, and pair of rubber gloves (alum is nontoxic but can be irritating to the skin), measure the alum for the dye bath. Using the scale, weigh out the amount of alum to equal 20 percent of the weight of the napkins. (In my case, this was approximately 75 grams.)

Transfer the alum to the clean and dry stockpot and add 1 cup (240 ml) boiling water to dissolve the alum. Add hot tap water to fill the pot almost to

Right: Before the fabric dyeing process begins, I pull the petals off the flowers and weigh them.

Below: The napkins are soaked in the dye bath with the flowers for twenty-four hours.

Right: After rinsing the wet napkins, I bring them outside and hang them to dry on the wires that support my raspberry bushes.

the top, making sure to leave enough room for the napkins. Clip the thermometer to the stockpot and place it over a hot plate. Add the rinsed napkins to the pot.

Heat the alum solution to 160°F (71°C) and maintain that temperature for about an hour (I keep my hot plate on setting 2 for this process). Use the candy thermometer to monitor the temperature. Turn off the heat and let the napkins soak in the alum solution for 24 hours, then remove them from the liquid with the tongs and rinse well in cold water.

Prepare the dye bath: Fill the second pot almost full with water and add flowers to equal the weight of the dry napkins (in my case, that was about 370 grams).

Heat the flower water to 120°F (49°C) for about an hour. If you're using marigolds, you don't want the water to boil, as this darkens the yellow. Turn off the heat and let the flowers soak overnight.

Dye the napkins: The next morning, you can either put the flower dye bath through a strainer to remove the petals or put the napkins into the flower dye pot with the flowers still in there. I left my flowers in the pot because I wanted some irregularity in the color—wherever the petals touch the cloth, the dye color will be stronger.

Submerge the napkins in the dye bath and heat the bath to 120°F (49°C). Again, to retain the brightness of the color, you don't want the water to boil. Let the pot heat for about an hour and then turn off the heat. Leave the napkins in the dye pot until the next day.

Remove the napkins from the dye pot and rinse in cool water. Hang them on a line to dry. When washing after each use, use a delicate detergent and the delicate cycle on your washing machine, or wash by hand.

Zinnias

I find the profile of zinnia flower heads and their geometric sequence of petals very intriguing and was first inspired to grow them after studying a 1915 photo by Charles Sheeler. I love the simple, graphic composition of his image, and I wanted to have zinnias to use in my own arrangements and still lifes as well.

Each spring, I plant an allée along the central stone path in the round garden with different types of zinnia flower heads and colors (see the list of favorites on page 188). I also include zinnias on the tennis court garden at the edges of the raised beds next to the marigolds, cosmos, calendulas, and nasturtiums. I want the zinnias to have good airflow and be able to stretch out over the bed edge if they need the room.

Zinnias are easy to plant, whether started indoors in pots in colder climates or by sowing the seeds directly in the ground after the soil has warmed (mid-May in my garden). The reward for your small bit of effort is a wonderful, vibrant display, in the garden and in the vase, where the blossoms last well once cut. Zinnia seeds can be collected in fall and saved for the following year.

Zinnias don't need much in the way of fertilizer or other soil amendments. And though they are generally foolproof, they do best with some staking or tying up, to keep their long stems upright.

Regular pruning should help produce more flowers and help keep the plants clean.

Unattractive powdery mildew and other fungal diseases can appear on zinnias for several reasons. Perhaps the plants are spaced too closely together and the leaves don't have enough airflow. In the round garden, I water with an overhead rain tower, and the moisture sitting on the leaves can start the mold reaction. Or after a wet summer, fungus and mold carried by the wind can land on the plants as autumn approaches. It is helpful to water the flowers in the early morning, so that the water has time to evaporate off the leaves by night.

I had just pulled the cobalt blue–and–white porcelain vase out of the kiln and cut this gorgeous salmon-colored zinnia from the garden when I took this photo as an homage to Charles Sheeler.

Zinnia and Nasturtium Leaves, Charles Sheeler, 1915.

Most times, I leave the plants alone, as they bloom just fine, but zinnias can be treated with organic Captain Jack's copper fungicide. (This will also work for dahlias if they develop powdery mildew.) I try to protect zinnias from slug damage by spreading diatomaceous earth in early spring or by using a plastic slug prevention ring.

Arranged on their own, zinnias make a joyful display; they pair beautifully with other annuals, including dahlias of all shapes and sizes.

FAVORITE VARIETIES

Zinnia elegans **'State Fair'** A pollinator favorite with large flower heads in classic red, white, yellow, and pink

Z. elegans **Benary's Giant Series** Easy-to-sow zinnias with large flower heads in powerful fall colors, including red, salmon, and lime green, on tall stems

Z. elegans **Cactus Flowered Mix** With quilled petals that seem to shake in vibrant colors

Z. elegans **'Queeny Lime Orange'** Vibrant apricot-colored petals that gradiate to lime around a rose center

Z. haageana **'Persian Carpet Mix'** Variegated patterns in gold, orange, burgundy, and yellow shades that combine to make brilliant bouquets

Z. **Oklahoma Series** A smaller variety in a great range of pinks, purples, and yellows that make great bloomers when regularly deadheaded

Z. **'Jazzy Mix'** Petite 1- to 2- inch (2.5 to 5 cm) flower heads in brightly striped orange, yellow, and red colors

Fire engine–red zinnias are in concert with marigolds and dahlias, in a pair of elegant white earthenware footed bowls. Nasturtiums trail over the sides of each, to dramatic effect.

Leaves That I Love

Japanese Maple, Coleus, Fig Leaves, Grape Leaves, Hosta, Kirengeshoma, Ferns, Smoke Bush, and Solomon's Seal

Foliage contributes an incredible variety of shapes, textures, and colors to nearly any arrangement of flowers in a vase. Once you start to look around the garden or even your yard, you will be amazed at how many wonderful leaves can be put to good use this way. When I'm perusing plants to buy at a nursery or online, I always look for unusual greenery that I haven't seen before.

Japanese maple leaves turn an intense maroon around the time that the jewel-toned chrysanthemums bloom. Using a flower frog, I placed them together in an oxblood-glazed porcelain bowl.

JAPANESE MAPLE

When we planted a Japanese maple (*Acer japonicum*) at least twenty-five years ago, we nestled it between the star magnolia and large rhododendrons at the front of the house. It should be moved to have more room, but it still manages to spread its branches and produce lovely red leaves in the current location. I wait until the nights are cool in fall and its leaves turn a brilliant red, then I cut some branches and use them in a vase with chrysanthemums, as both shrub and flower are native to China and Japan. The tree takes little maintenance other than a once-yearly application of fertilizer in early spring.

COLEUS

I love coleus for their range of foliage colors, from dark red to electric green. The plants can be purchased in spring, but it's also a good idea to pick up those that are left behind at the nurseries in late summer or early fall, when prices are marked down; they may be rootbound in their small plastic pots but are otherwise usually in fine health. I pull them out of their pots, cut off the bottom of each root (anywhere from ½ to 1 inch/1.3 to 2.5 cm), and give them a great drink of water before transplanting them directly in the soil, where they stretch out to fill in holes where other plants haven't performed so exuberantly. (I tuck coleus plants under roses or dahlias that haven't properly filled out, for example.) They aren't fussy about being planted in the shade or full sun; once settled in, coleus grows beautifully until the first frost.

Oftentimes I will take a cutting off the top of a plant before frost, root it in water, and transplant the rooted sprout to a terra-cotta pot inside, where it's warmer. Or you can simply dig up an entire plant before frost and plunk it into a clay pot. With a little fertilizer added to the watering can, the plants will do nicely all winter long and be ready to go back into the garden in spring.

FIG LEAVES

I have two fig trees: one that has lived in a large pot for about ten years and a winter-hardy one that I planted more recently in the ground, against the greenhouse, where it gets warm sun most of the day. I hope that the latter can grow large and produce an abundance of foliage and fruit. In August and September, when the dark purple figs are ripe, I cut the branches and use them in arrangements, especially in bowls, with the leaves draping over the edges.

GRAPE LEAVES

My grapevine is planted in a bed on the old tennis court, next to a tall fence that supports it as it grows. The grape I chose is ostensibly for eating, but because the vine is so tall, it's hard to reach the fruit. (The birds eat the grapes anyway, unless I pick them when they're very green.) I mostly use the vines for arrangements: I place them in a bowl with flowers that bloom at the same moment, such as sunflowers and rudbeckias.

HOSTA

When we built our barn a couple of decades ago, the first thing I planted

was a row of *Hosta sieboldiana* 'Elegans' on the side of the stone walkway that leads to the front door. I love the drama of the broad blue-green leaves that grow enormous by early summer. 'Aureomarginata' and 'Tokudama Flavocircinalis' hostas, plant gifts from friends, grow around the sides of the barn and in the shady part of the round garden. We have to be vigilant about spraying the hostas that line the stone driveway with organic deer repellent, otherwise the leaves are a perfect dessert for the deer in the evening. I use the leaves when they are at their most vibrant to form the base of arrangements. Late in autumn, before and even after a frost, the hostas turn a yellow ocher color, which pairs perfectly with some of the chrysanthemums.

KIRENGESHOMA

Around twenty years ago, I was given a kirengeshoma, or yellow wax bells (*Kirengeshoma palmata*), by a friend. Now it lives in the shady side of the round garden and is about 4 by 4 feet (1.2 by 1.2 m). The herbaceous perennial is part of the Hydrangeaceae family and native to Japan and China. In Japanese, *ki* means "yellow," *renge* means "lotus blossom," and *shoma* means "hat." I love kirengeshoma because of the waxy flowers that open from late August to early September in a shade of yellow that blends perfectly with the dahlias and zinnias that bloom at the same time. The

'French Quarter', 'Trusty Rusty', and other coleus
Ostrich fern
Solomon's seal

Common fig
Purple grapes vine
Smoke bush

'Elegans' hosta
Japanese maple
Kirengeshoma

flower clusters of three to five panicles drooping on a stem stand out against the large palmate leaves. I like to cut branches and place them in a vase first, as support for the flowers to follow.

FERNS

Ferns are herbaceous, vascular plants whose leaves (or fronds) reproduce through spores. I think about their long history on earth (they are known to have existed as far back as nearly 360 million years ago). A vast bank of ferns in front of the tennis court thrived there long before we moved to the property. I am cheered by the freshness these bright green fronds deliver, even in the hottest part of summer. After a frost, they turn brown and lie down, offering a wonderful habitat for insects and birds during the colder season. In the round garden, I planted silver Japanese painted ferns (*Athyrium niponicum*), which have traveled outside the fence and appeared in the beds around the building where I keep my gas kiln. An evergreen Christmas fern (*Polystichum acrostichoides*) against my studio does not die back in autumn; I use its fronds to bring texture to holiday arrangements.

Just before the first frost, as the ferns outside the tennis court change from green to nut brown in color, I like to combine them with fruit-laden apple branches in a marbleized terra-cotta urn.

SMOKE BUSH

The cuttings from smoke bush (*Cotinus coggyria*)—both the leaves and the feathery flowers that conjure the image of smoke and, therefore, the name—add wonderful texture and drama to floral arrangements. I purchased one of the drought-tolerant plants fifteen years ago and planted it just outside the tennis court fence, where it blooms from late May until August. If I need to prune the bush, I wait until after the bloom finishes, which gives it time to set up buds for the next year. The cuttings pair well with dahlias and can also be dried and saved to use as accents in arrangements of chrysanthemums.

SOLOMON'S SEAL

I have Solomon's seal (*Polygonatum odoratum* var. *pluriflorum*) in several places: in the round garden, down by the witch hazels, and at the side of the house with a bank of tall ferns. This easy-to-grow woodland plant is happiest in the shadier areas of the yard, as long as the soil is moist. It is planted as a rhizome; once established, it spreads freely. When it has finished blooming, it produces berries that the birds seem to love. The leaves are formed on long, upright stems, and the flowers are small, dangling, bell-shaped clusters. I cut the stems and use them in a vase along with tulips that bloom at the same time, keeping the arrangement simple so that the Solomon's seal's flowers are plainly visible.

PART V

AUTUMNAL

THERE'S NOTHING TERRIBLY SUBDUED OR
retiring about the cutting gardens from mid-September through
the end of October. These weeks mark the traditional harvest
season, when several flowers are in bloom, including my beloved
dahlias. To me, an armful of freshly cut dahlias represents the
beauty of autumn. These and many of the other seasonal
blossoms are quite hale and hearty, with rich, bold colors and
endlessly fascinating and complex petal formations. I enjoy
sending visitors home with bundles of them all, to share in the
bounty. The developments in the garden are not unlike what's
happening on the trees at the same moment; the leaves put on
such a wondrous display that we have no choice but to pause to
admire them before they drop off the trees.

Toward the end of October, I think about closing the garden.
As we experience our first frost, I know that shortly it will be
time, depending on the weather, to start digging out the dahlia
tubers and organizing them for storage in the barn basement. I
tend to leave the dead plant material in the garden for the birds,
insects, and other wildlife over the colder months to follow.

Dahlias

It's been a few decades since I began growing dahlias. And yet, I still can't get enough of them. In fact, the flowers and my pottery have become so intertwined in my life's work that it's impossible for me to imagine one without the other. Each growing season, I produce an abundant harvest of these incredibly joyous flowers to arrange in my pots and photograph in the studio. You might think I'd get bored photographing them year after year, but the opposite is true.

For about ten years, I have taught a class called Dauntless Dahlias at the New York Botanical Garden. My goal is to illustrate how easy the flowers are to grow, and to encourage gardeners of all experience levels to do so. When it comes to choosing dahlias, I prefer to think abstractly rather than specifically, and to include both the classics and new-to-me varieties in a range of colors, sizes, shapes, and petal formations. I try not to obsess over the names (and get a bit flummoxed when people ask me to identify them). If you can't find the exact one you've seen in another garden or on social media, don't worry—the world of dahlias is so

At the height of the autumnal season, an abundant array of plant life—including dahlias, coleus leaves, salvias, zinnias, late roses, nasturtiums, Japanese anemones, tomato vines, and asters—fills a trio of footed marbleized cups. The composition is inspired by Dutch still life paintings.

vast and exciting, there's always another that will delight you in equal measure. On pages 202–203, the flowers shown are categorized by the shape of the petal, including decorative, informal decorative, cactus, peony, and so on, to demonstrate the wide range of colors and sizes available within it. Recent years have seen a vast expansion of farms selling dahlia tubers; however, the companies I've been using from the beginning are still reliable sources (see page 280).

HOW TO GROW DAHLIAS

Dahlias are truly among the most approachable flowers for growing, requiring little more than a sunny spot in the garden with healthy, organic soil.

My best advice is to get a good staking system in place before you begin. I use tomato cages, but a DIY arrangement of bamboo stakes in a triangular formation secured with biodegradable twine can provide adequate support for the plants as they grow and may, admittedly, be more attractive. If deer are a problem where you live, you'll want to find a way to protect the flowers (and the tubers), such as fencing.

Dahlia planting season kicks off for me in mid to late April with the unboxing of the tubers in the basement. Many have been stored since I pulled them out of the ground the previous November, while others are recent purchases. First, I check to see if the

tubers have eyes (like those on a potato), which indicate their readiness to grow again. I wait until the heavy April rains are over, around the second week of May, before I plant the tubers. It takes a good two weeks for me to get all the dahlias in the ground, and I am grateful if friends come over to help.

To promote profuse harvests, I first pinch the center bud of each stem when

The variegated cream- and pink-colored blooms held in two celadon pitchers include 'Otto's Thrill', 'Vera Seyfang', and 'Pinelands Princess' dahlias; 'Sally Holmes' roses; and 'Tower Chamois China' asters. For the photograph, I wanted the pots to melt into a backdrop to bring the flower shapes into relief.

FAVORITE VARIETIES

Dahlia **'Bishop of Llandaff'** Extra-exuberant semidouble scarlet petals and dark purple leaves

D. **'Bodacious'** Flashy, bright orange petals and yellow undersides

D. **'Café au Lait'** The darling of modern weddings (and Instagram), with whispery, barely perceptible peach or pink tones

D. **'Clyde's Choice'** A dinner plate–size orange-peach dahlia that is a vigorous grower and prolific bloomer

D. **'Devil du Roi Albert'** A prolific heirloom variety that stores well over the winter

D. **'Juanita'** A rich red cactus type that reaches 6 inches (15 cm) in diameter

D. **'Meadowburn Old Tweet'** A Meadowburn Farm heirloom yellow peony type first bred in the early 1900s that grows up to 8 feet (2.4 m) tall

D. **'Myrtle's Brandy'** Excellent for cutting, with lots of white-tipped red petals and good stem length

D. **'Paul Smith'** A dark red ball type on the smaller side, with beautiful petal formation

D. **'Spartacus'** A giant, with velvety black-red flowers

D. **'Walter Hardisty'** A large white, fluffy, dinner-plate variety that blooms late in the season; too beautiful not to have every year despite stems that aren't great for cutting

Decorative types, including 'Hamari Gold', 'Kidd's Climax', 'Mrs. I de Ver Warner', 'Myrtle's Brandy', 'Spartacus', 'Tartan', and 'Thomas A. Edison'

Cactus types, including 'Inland Dynasty', 'Pinelands Princess', and 'Preference'
Waterlily, orchid, and peony types, including (respectively) 'Debora Renae',
    'Honka', 'Bishop of York'

Ball types, including 'Audrey Grace', 'Cornell', 'Golden Scepter', and 'Lupin Ben'
Informal decorative types, including 'Elsie Huston', 'Jane Cowl', and 'Labyrinth'

it reaches 6 to 12 inches (15 to 30 cm) high. Then, once the plant is producing flower buds, I give it another pinch, this time removing the lateral buds and leaving just the main bud; this method (known as disbudding) will produce a longer stem, which is useful for cutting and arranging. To fertilize, I dilute organic fish emulsion with water and spray the plants every two weeks or so in summer. (This same mixture seems to benefit all the plants in the garden.)

In an average year, the dahlias begin blooming around mid-July and continue over the next several months. I liken the display to a symphony, with a riotous crescendo of blooms from late August well into October, depending on mercurial weather patterns. (In warmer climates, they can keep going for several weeks longer.)

As soon as the first frost hits, it's time to cut the dahlias back and dig out the tubers. If my schedule allows, I wait a week or two after the plants turn black from frost, though many years the frost arrives so late that I dig the tubers out

before then. (The dates of things like frost are increasingly hard to predict, due to climate change.) To prep the tubers for winter storage, I cut the stems down to 2 or 3 inches (5 or 7.5 cm) and brush off the soil before bringing them into the basement. I spread them out to dry for anywhere from a few days to two weeks before shaking them once again to remove the remaining dirt and finally packing them in cardboard cartons with wood shavings to protect them from rot.

HOW TO ARRANGE DAHLIAS

I cut dahlias early in the morning. No special conditioning is necessary because the fresh-cut flowers are already hardy and should last five to seven days in the vase.

Dahlias can be combined with zinnias, cosmos, marigolds, flowering herbs—nearly anything, really. I like to combine groups of dahlias in similar colors or variations of one color. An extra-large ombré design is a particular favorite.

THE BEAUTY IN THE CHAOS

My gardens were originally and primarily designed to grow dahlias, my first flower love. Over the years, however, other blooms have become equally important to me, and gradually the emphasis on what I grow has shifted, though I don't have a clear record of which plants I've added over the years, or of how many of them (neither my garden nor my studio is neat or orderly). I'm not particularly good at keeping track of the seeds, bulbs, plugs, and trees that I buy online or in plant nurseries. My only excuse for this is a lack of organization and an unwillingness to spend the time necessary to keep a running record. I'd much rather devote that time to sitting at the wheel or arranging flowers in the pots. A friend recently suggested that I print receipts for all of my plant purchases and file them in a notebook, so I can document the history of the cutting gardens. This would also serve as an easy way to know what to expect when the plant boxes start showing up. This year, I am going to try this method of recordkeeping.

Yet and still, a part of me continues to embrace the beauty in the garden chaos that ensues every year. I feel that somehow I will find the correct spot for the flower or shrub when it comes time to plant it. Because I generally keep such poor records, I leave tags at the base of the annual plants so that I can identify the variety once their flowers bloom, and so that the following season I can be sure to plant them where they will be happiest and produce the most flowers for cutting and arranging.

This improvisational nature energizes me, and I love to watch the garden come together as a unit. I have a vague plan when putting individual plants into a very jammed garden bed, but I also wait to see what plants emerge in spring and work around them. I look to see where things have self-seeded and try to gauge how the weather has affected everything.

The gardens reach their crescendo in September. Even when it looks like there's no room to be had, I can always find a corner in the raised beds to accommodate an herb or something else from a plant nursery. If I need to expand a border to hold a peony bush, I dig out a new section. I work very hard to have everything look its best for the Garden Conservancy's Open Days annual tour in mid-September. If a dahlia hasn't done as well as I hoped, however, or there is an empty spot in the garden, I will move a potted geranium there or go to a nursery and purchase another plant, such as a canna, coleus, or Japanese anemone, and place it there. Things work out in the end every year, which serves as an affirmation of sorts for letting nature run its often chaotic, ever beautiful course.

Chrysanthemums

The chrysanthemum is among the longest lasting of all cut flowers, which helps explain its popularity the world over. Native to China, chrysanthemums were cultivated as far back as the fifteenth century BCE. The flowers were steeped to make tea, and the greens enjoyed in salads. Chrysanthemums were also thought to cure headaches. In the seventh and eighth centuries, the flowers migrated to Japan, where they were highly prized and trained into beautiful forms.

I first truly appreciated the beauty of chrysanthemums at the annual kiku exhibition held at the New York Botanical Garden in mid-autumn. *Kiku* is the Japanese word for "chrysanthemum," as well as for the centuries-old art form of carefully clipped plants trained for display. It takes a year or more to create each dramatic exhibition. At the NYBG, resident horticulturists work with a group of specialist Japanese gardeners to learn the art of pruning and training different chrysanthemum varieties to grow, controlling sunlight and pinching back some stems to concentrate the plant's energy on others. Though I have not attempted a kiku display of my own, the offerings at NYBG continue to inspire me to plant new varieties of mums and to find ways to capture their singular beauty in my arrangements and photographs.

The first year, I planted them directly into the raised beds. Unfortunately, this was not a good idea, as the plants were difficult to prune in that location during the growing months, and the flowers cannot withstand a hard frost. The following year, I resolved to keep the mums in flowerpots that could be easily moved inside for the cold season.

The second year was slightly more successful, but I did make another important discovery. In my enthusiasm, I had gone overboard with the number of plants, and it was nearly impossible to care for them all properly. More is definitely not always more in the garden. I made every effort to stake and pinch the buds to encourage each plant to focus on a few strong blooms, as the kiku masters do. When the first frost was expected, I brought the pots into my studio—and I was surrounded by the flowers. It was a bit chaotic. I resolved to try moderation the next season.

As I write this, I'm currently in my fourth season growing a variety of heirloom chrysanthemums. There are many different classifications of chrysanthemums, but I gravitate to the irregular incurve, intermediate incurve, anemone, and spider types. Last year went well, but I did not pinch the stems or keep removing extra buds (see page 213), and the stems flopped over with lots of

The exquisite petal formations of chrysanthemums inspire contemplation. In this wood-fired, ash-glazed vase, 'Jefferson Park', 'Luxor', and 'Flair' varieties appear majestic but are a bit upstaged by the madcap brush-and-thistle type 'Aoi' on the right side.

'Savanna Charlton'   'Apricot Alexis'   'Norton Vic'
'Mocha'   'Jefferson Park'   'Hagomoro'
'Lili Gallon'   'Crimson Tide'   'Flair'

small, albeit lovely, blooms. This year, I will try to have the large Japanese style of single-stem chrysanthemum heads that are so exquisite.

After seeing spectacular perennial chrysanthemums in the cutting garden at Chanticleer in Wayne, Pennsylvania, I decided to try some of these myself this coming spring. The winter-hardy plants do not need to be brought into the greenhouse during the cold months. I was told that cutting these specific chrysanthemums back to 6 inches (15 cm) around the end of May would make the bushes fuller, with more flowers.

HOW TO GROW CHRYSANTHEMUMS

Plant chrysanthemums, both heirloom and perennial, in a sunny spot, with at least five hours of sunlight a day, and ensure good drainage in their pots or garden bed. Water when the soil is dry and not from overhead, which would wet the leaves and blooms and perhaps invite mold. Chrysanthemums require a good amount of space for ample airflow— this will discourage mold as well. If the purchased plant is in a plastic pot with cramped roots, it should be repotted into a larger container and the roots freshly cut a couple of inches (5 cm) from the bottom to allow adequate room to grow. Pinching the stems and continually removing extra buds is essential to promoting the growth of large blooms, and deadheading and removing old leaves encourages new

blooms and keeps the plant vibrant. It is also important to note that the flower color will vary according to region, average temperature, and climate.

HOW TO ARRANGE CHRYSANTHEMUMS

I arrange chrysanthemums depending on the type I am growing. If it's a variety that has one to three blooms on a stem, I often just place it in a vase that can handle a single stem, to give both the flower and the pot full attention. If a more abundant arrangement is in order, chrysanthemums can be paired with other late-blooming beauties such as Japanese anemones, red and blue blackberries, and colorful hostas or maples.

This year, I have planted perennial chrysanthemums, which will be fuller and bushier in form, and serve as the foundation for bouquets.

FAVORITE VARIETIES

Chrysanthemum **'Cheerleader'** An impressively sized mum with deep golden amber petals that curve inward

C. **'Coral Reef'** A large spider mum with coral, orange, and gold petals

C. **'Derek Bircumshaw'** A brilliant yellow with a strong growth pattern

C. **'Drummer Boy'** A tall cushion-style mum with large flower heads of scarlet petals

C. **'Heather James'** Two-toned flower heads with bronze-and-red florets

C. **'Jefferson Park'** A deep purple variety with great form

C. **'River City'** The most beautiful salmon color

Pollinator Species

Goldenrod, Salvia, Milkweed, Bee Balm, Joe-Pye Weed,
Helianthus, Ageratum, Hyssop, Vernonia

For the past few years, I have been adding more native plants to the perimeter of the round garden and to the raised beds on the old tennis court. Pollinators—insects, bees, butterflies, and birds—gravitate to these flowers for their sustenance and, in turn, contribute in no small part to a more healthy, biodiverse environment.

I have also observed that the pollinating insects, bees, and butterflies seem to like the roses, dahlias, and annuals equally well, which assures me that I have made a wonderful feast of flowers for them. Beyond their beneficial uses in the garden, I plant late-season pollinator species because I like to mix many of them in with the flowers in my arrangements, especially some of the beautifully colored flowers like salvia, ageratum, and goldenrod, and the unusually textured varieties including milkweed and bee balm.

Pollinator plants are highly adaptable and luxuriate in the organic earth of my raised beds. If allowed, however, they would overtake the rest of the flowers that I have carefully placed, so a fair amount of editing and extracting (aka weeding) is required during the summer months to keep them in check.

GOLDENROD

Goldenrod, or *Solidago*, is naturally abundant around the edges of our property. It has found its way into the cracks and beds of both cutting gardens, where I remove it by the roots when it becomes too enthusiastic. This herbaceous perennial, native to North America as part of the aster family, has more than 120 cultivars. *Solidago* derives from the Latin word *solidus*, which means "to make whole," as the plant was used medicinally by Indigenous populations. The common name, goldenrod, relates to the color and shape of the blooms, which appear at the end of a long, bending stem.

I rely on goldenrod to provide pollen for the native bees and honeybees at the end of summer and well into autumn, especially if the weather has been dry. For bouquets, I strip the leaves, cut the stems short, and use the blooms as a base to hold successive flowers in place.

Goldenrod stems provide a foundation and peek out from beneath a grouping that includes 'Kelvin Floodlight', 'Clyde's Choice', 'Maniac', and 'Bishop of York' dahlias, as well as hydrangeas and nasturtiums. The wispiness of the small goldenrod flowers contrasts with the solidity of the heartier blooms.

Vernonia
Goldenrod
Joe-pye weed

Milkweed
Hyssop
Bee balm

Ageratum
'Black and Blue' salvia
Helianthus

Goldenrod drapes languidly over the side of a bowl or vase, to dramatic effect. And I so love the deep yellow color of the flowers that I've used the plant in both fresh and dried states as a natural dye for linen (see page 183 for a napkin project).

SALVIA

I first came to admire ornamental salvias in Napa, California, where my family and I vacationed every summer when our children were young. Salvia blooms there abundantly, pretty much all year long, but here in Connecticut, the plant behaves as an annual. It does not like the freezing, damp winter, so I cultivate new plants every spring. Salvia is widely available in seed form and can be started six to eight weeks before the date of the last frost, but I have more success with more mature salvia plants that go straight into my garden beds. My local nurseries offer a great selection. I like these plants' wonderful scents as well as their deer resistance.

There are four main species of ornamental annual salvias, which are all part of the mint family: *Salvia coccinea*, *S. farinacea*, *S. splendens*, and *S. patens*. These salvias generally grow from 2 to 5 feet (61 to 152 cm) tall. When the flower heads are open, I cut their long stems down at the base of the plant and use the flowers, especially the blue types, as accents or exclamation points in a bouquet, where they are hardy enough to last for about a week in a vase.

MILKWEED

When it's in season, early to mid summer, I see common milkweed (*Asclepias syriaca*) lining the road near my home on my morning walks. I strive to have some of my own because it provides a crucial habitat for the monarch butterfly (which lays its eggs on the leaves), hosts many other pollinating insects and birds, and improves the quality of soil by adding nitrogen as the plant dies back. The common name for this plant derives from the milky sap that it secretes, especially when cut; *asclepias* comes from the ancient Greek for "swallow-wort." The sap is also toxic to many insects, so it is useful for pest control in gardens. At the moment, there's not a huge amount of milkweed around my beds, and what

FAVORITE SALVIA VARIETIES

Salvia coccinea Scarlet sage, with a red flower that is especially appealing to hummingbirds

S. farinacea '**Blue Bedder**' A mealycup sage cultivar known for its tall spikes and deep blue flowers

S. farinacea '**Fairy Queen**' Another mealycup sage with blue-and-white flowers on long stalks and a lengthy bloom window

S. patens Boasts especially gorgeous blue blossoms

S. splendens Scarlet or saucy sage, with spikes covered in deep red flowers

S. uliginosa Called bog sage, with tall, slender stems topped with deep sky-blue flowers with splotches of white in the centers

S. '**Amistad**' Tall, spiky plants with deep purple flowers with black calyces; a favorite of hummingbirds

S. '**Wendy's Wish**' Hot pink–magenta, tube-shaped flowers on maroon-colored stems

It is nice to feature flowers that I usually employ for
underpinnings as the focus of a bouquet. Here goldenrod,
asters, geranium leaves, mountain mint, Queen Anne's
lace, Japanese anemone, hyacinth bean, and morning
glories fill seven marbleized vases.

is there doesn't seem to spread madly (as some gardeners complain that it does). Nevertheless, I am grateful that it reappears in the garden each year. I use milkweed sparingly in bouquets because of the sap, which gets all over my hands, but sometimes I can't resist showing off one or two of its beautiful flower heads in a vase.

BEE BALM

Bee balm (*Monarda*), also known as wild bergamot or monarda, is another pollinator favorite. Hummingbirds, bees, and butterflies reach down the flower heads' long, tubular petals to access nectar; later in fall, the dried seed heads attract resident birds. The genus name *Monarda* is in honor of the sixteenth-century Spanish botanist Nicolás Monardes, and *bergamot* refers to the perennial flower's fragrance, which is reminiscent of the oranges of the same name. I have a red and a lavender monarda in the garden, which I bought as plants and use in my arrangements.

JOE-PYE WEED

Purple joe-pye weed (*Eutrochium purpureum*) blooms from late August through September. Legend has it that Joe Pye was an Indigenous medicine man who traveled around New England using wildflowers to cure diseases. This pollinator grows in my round garden and just outside of it, along the border, where it is beloved by the butterflies.

Though it's said to be deer resistant, I have seen deer feasting on the long stems in summertime. Drought tolerant and unfussy about soil, joe-pye weed is available as seed or as a plant at nurseries that specialize in native flowers, which is how I began to grow it.

HELIANTHUS

An easy, drought- and deer-resistant pollinator plant that blooms from the end of summer until just before frost, helianthus is a favorite with the butterflies, bees, and insects. There are over seventy species of this perennial flower, which is native to Mexico, but I have found the *Helianthus microcephalus* 'Lemon Queen' sunflower happiest in both of my cutting gardens as well as along the border where the spring-blooming witch hazel and viburnum shrubs are planted. The name is derived from the Greek *helios*, meaning "sun," and *anthos*, meaning "flower." It's not to be confused with the more commonly known sunflower, however. The difference between an annual (see page 164) and a perennial sunflower is that the former will grow, bloom, and die in one season's cycle, whereas a perennial sunflower grown from seed will not flower for two years. It establishes roots and rhizomes and then will return each year, most likely taller and wider, with a splendid display of deep yellow flowers that can grow to a height of 8 to 10 feet (2 to 3 m). Once cut, helianthus combines beautifully with the acid-yellow dahlias and zinnias from my cutting garden.

AGERATUM

The perennial version of ageratum (*Eupatorium coelestinum*) grows in both of my cutting gardens and returns every spring, unlike the annual ageratum, *Ageratum houstonianum*. It has made itself quite comfortable in the raised beds that get more shade in the afternoon. I prize the unusual blue color of the late-season flower, which is a member of the daisy family and consists of dense clusters of tiny florets at the top of a 2-foot-long (61 cm) stem. The word *ageratum* is derived from the Greek *ageras*, meaning "nonaging," as the flower blooms for a couple of months. I purchase ageratum in a pot, but it is also available from seed and tends to volunteer, too. I like to use it in small-scale bouquets where it can provide soft pops of blue.

HYSSOP

Anise hyssop (*Agastache foeniculum*) was one of the first perennials I planted in the raised beds on the former tennis court. The name *agastache* derives from the Greek words *ágan*, meaning "very much," and *stákhus*, meaning "ear of grain," which describes the 3-foot-tall (1 m) spikes of purple flowers and toothed leaves. *Hyssop* comes from the Greek *hyssopos*. It has a strong licorice scent and is another beautiful color to have in autumn for bouquets. The plant is edible and can be used in baking and salads, where it adds notes of mint and anise (some find it slightly citrusy). Hyssop thrives in full sun or partial shade, where it will flower reliably from late summer through frost. I purchased my hyssop as plants, but you can grow it from seed. It will also spread around the garden and find new spots on its own, which I appreciate.

VERNONIA

Vernonia fasciculata, more commonly known as ironweed, stands about 8 feet (2.4 m) tall in the tennis court garden and lives quite happily along the fringes of the round garden. The flowers gather in bunches at the top of the long branches and tower over nearby dahlias, roses, and other seasonal blooms. Its rich, purple-blue hue adds a welcome punch to the surroundings when it blooms, usually from late August or September until the first frost. Vernonia is named for the British botanist William Vernon, and *fasciculata* comes from the Latin *fasciculus*, meaning "bunch of flowers." Vernonia is a butterfly magnet, and I love to sit nearby and watch the insects flutter about on the high tops. I don't cut this one as much as some of the other native pollinators, as the hairy stems are a bit rough to handle.

Asters

A few years ago, while searching for a plant to provide a bit of blue color in the autumn palette, I read about asters in an article on late-season gardens. Soon after, I made room in the garden for these easy-to-grow perennials. It turns out that the native aster, which blooms continuously from autumn until frost, was just the flower I needed. It is part of the Asteraceae family, which comprises more than 180 aster species. The common name comes from the Greek word for "star," specifically referring to the goddess Astraea (aka the starry maid), who wept when she realized there were no stars on earth. Her tears created the star-shaped flowers.

I have purchased varieties in a great range of blues, but asters are also available in pink, purple, and white. Wherever I choose to plant them, the flowers perform beautifully; they also eagerly volunteer themselves around the garden. I let them go where they wish, as they fit right in with my efforts to weave more natives into the beds of dahlias and other late-summer and early-autumn bloomers. Their yellow centers provide a wonderful contrast to the reds and oranges of many zinnias and dahlias as well as complement the myriad yellow flowers throughout the garden.

Asters can be started from seed, though they are readily available as nursery plants in early spring. A more mature plant allows for a better show in fall, but asters do fill out quickly, as long as they are happy in their location. They are resistant to deer and other rodents, unfussy about soil, and able to thrive in full sun or partial shade. You often see them growing in abundance on roadsides and in meadows, seemingly without much intervention or routine care. The tops of aster plants can be chopped off in May or June if a shorter, bushier shape is the goal, but I usually let them get long and leggy.

I like to cut the flowers short and use them at the base of an arrangement to support other flowers like dahlias, Japanese anemones, zinnias, and late-summer roses. I often use coleus leaves with them, too.

Despite its small size, the New England aster is the star of the show in this footed bowl. Along with a few coleus leaves, they hold up 'Wekmerewby' (Grande Dame) roses; 'Spartacus', 'Thomas A. Edison', and 'Emory Paul' dahlias; red and pink zinnias; and raspberry branches.

FAVORITE VARIETIES

Aster ageratoides **'Ezo Murasaki'** A late-blooming, daisylike Asian variety with bright violet petals and yellow centers

A. **'Cotswold Gem'** A hybridized, compact-growth, starry aster with light pinkish-purplish petals

Symphyotrichum lateriflorum **'Lady in Black'** A cultivar of the native wildflower with a rose-colored center surrounded by white, daisylike petals and deep purple, nearly black leaves

S. novae-angliae The New England aster; known for its large flower heads in a wide range of pinks and purples

Amaranths

Amaranth flowers are a bit of an enigma. In the garden and in the vase, they manage to look at once elegant and unruly, abundant and spare, common and exceptional.

You may be familiar with amaranth as a grain; its seeds and leaves have been grown for centuries as a food source, and when ground into flour, it serves as a gluten-free alternative to wheat flours. The Aztecs, among other ancient civilizations across the continents, grew amaranth as a principal crop. But the plant is prized as an annual ornamental in the garden as well, particularly its most well-known variety, love-lies-bleeding (*Amaranthus caudatus*).

I was searching for plants to arrange with my dark red dahlias in the pots, and the deep garnet, velvety blossoms of blood amaranth (*A. cruentus*) fit the bill. Since the seeds weren't available commercially in North American catalogs at the time, I ordered them from the British supplier Thompson & Morgan. Now just about every North American seed catalog carries amaranth in a range of colors and heights, which is a bit of a blessing and a curse: The wider the availability, the harder it is to control myself when it comes time to place an order.

Love-lies-bleeding was very popular in bouquets in Victorian times; its name is meant to represent the hopelessness of love. The medium-red seed head droops beautifully as it grows in the garden and looks especially dramatic as it falls over the edge of a vase. *A.* 'Hopi Red Dye' can reach 7 feet (2 m) tall, with gorgeous, black-red flower heads that stay erect as they grow. *A. cruentus* 'Hot Biscuits', another favorite, is shorter yet sturdy enough to support birds sitting on its large seed heads and branches. Its deep ocher pairs beautifully with late-summer colors of zinnias, dahlias, and rudbeckias; it's often used as a natural dye for fabrics, too.

I make sure to plant several varieties of amaranth every spring, throwing the seeds over the garden beds or sowing them in small biodegradable pots that I then transfer into the ground. Though they are annuals, they often volunteer, faithfully reseeding the next year in a new location. I readily welcome such surprises and keep an eye out for their small leaves in the soil (the 'Hopi Red Dye' leaflets are the easiest to spot). Once the flowers have bloomed, I keep the branches long and use them in the vase to support less-sturdy flower stems. Even after some flower heads are cut, the amaranths continue growing until the first frost. I so appreciate them for enhancing my late-summer and autumn arrangements.

Tendrils of ruby-red love-lies-bleeding (*Amaranthus caudatus*) drape from a horn-shaped vase as they glow in the early-morning light. Their leaves and stems, along with fig leaves, provide support for dahlias and roses.

An extravaganza of flowers explodes in a great autumn crescendo in this two-spouted vase. The seasonal blooms include 'Hot Biscuits' amaranths, Japanese anemones, and 'Zorro', 'Spartacus', 'Duet', 'Debora Renae', and 'Mrs. I. de Ver Warner' dahlias.

'Coral Fountain'
'Velvet Curtains'

'Hopi Red Dye'
'Hot Biscuits'

Japanese Anemones

I adore Japanese anemones, especially in autumn bouquets; the blossoms work beautifully with the dahlias, chrysanthemums, and other late bloomers in the cutting gardens. Their slender stems don't bend, which allows them to stand on their own, even in the breeze (their name comes from the Greek for "wind flower"), or to tower above other blossoms in a mixed bouquet. For this reason, I usually place them first or last in the arrangement. They can provide excellent support to the flowers that follow, or can serve as wonderful accents.

Native to China, the plants migrated to Japan, where they were also prized by Europeans in the seventeenth century. They are herbaceous perennials, meaning their upper leaves die back in autumn while the roots remain alive; the leaves sprout again in spring. I have several varieties of Japanese anemone that bloom in late July and later ones that flower until frost. Once they've established themselves in a semishaded spot with well-draining soil, the plants invariably grow larger each subsequent year. If a stem is cut, it does not regrow, but each plant provides many stems, so there are plenty of opportunities for cutting. I have put Japanese anemone plants in different parts of both cutting gardens to ensure a good supply of these graceful flowers.

The long, sturdy stems are topped by delicate florets in a translucent white, pale pink, or deep rose. My favorites are *Anemone hupehensis* 'Praecox', a deep pink and the earliest to bloom; *A. hupehensis* var. *japonica* 'Pamina', another deep pink beauty; *A.* × *hybrida* 'Honorine Jobert', an ethereal white that blooms later in September; and *A.* × *hybrida* 'Whirlwind', which features fluttery white petals with a deep yellow center.

Left and opposite: The Japanese anemones 'Honorine Jobert' and 'Pamina', which live together in the shadiest corner of the round garden, are the last flowers to bloom. When they are done, I leave their skeleton forms in place to view over the winter. The frilly petals of 'Pamina' connect with the decorative details on this group of earthenware bowls.

Bright, cheerful Japanese anemones make the transition from the raised beds to the vase quite easily; here the 'Honorine Jobert' variety mingles with dahlias, roses, and white asters in a beautifully muted assortment of porcelain bisque vases.

MAKING PRESSED-FLOWER CARDS

Saving flowers through drying and flattening has intrigued botanical gatherers for centuries. Archaeologists found pressed laurels in the three-thousand-year-old tomb of Tutankhamen's mother. In the sixteenth century, the Japanese developed oshibana, the art of pressed flowers, to create dried compositions, and when trade with Japan expanded in the 1800s, flower pressing became fashionable across the European continent and the United Kingdom. Centuries later, dried-flower images still resonate: When I was designing the card with pressed flowers at right, for instance, William Henry Fox Talbot's nineteenth-century fern calotypes and Josef Albers's leaf studies from the 1940s came to mind. Though different, both techniques beautifully celebrate the silhouette of the plant.

I've experimented with different methods of flower pressing over the years. Older methods include using a wooden flower press, or sandwiching flowers between copier paper and cardboard and placing the packet between heavy books, but it can take weeks for the flowers to dry. I have achieved the best results with the Microfleur press, which uses a microwave (or a sunny window) to dry flowers quickly and retains their bright colors beautifully (the Max option setting works better for larger flowers). If a flower press catches your fancy, however, I recommend trying one of the newer versions, such as the Gardener's Press, available from various online retailers. Whatever method you choose, this fairly simple, quick craft is fun to do with children of all ages when you have an abundance of flowers in bloom.

Tools & Materials

Fresh botanicals

Towel (optional)

Blank acid-free, cold-press folding watercolor cards with envelopes

Watercolor paint (I like Winsor & Newton sets for the variety of colors)

Newspaper, to keep your workstation tidy

Microfleur flower press or other press

Flat watercolor paintbrush

Round watercolor paintbrush

Mug or cup filled with water, for painting

Matte glue (I like the nontoxic Perfect Paper Adhesive brand)

2-inch (5 cm) paper clips

Select flowers and leaves: Look for blooms that can be pressed fairly flat. Anemones, roses, dahlias, and borage all work well for pressing. You can also find ferns and leaves on a walk or in the garden. Choose a few stems for each card you plan to make.

Ensure everything is dry: Place any damp blooms or leaves on a towel to dry as much as possible. You don't want too much time to elapse between the picking and the pressing, as the leaves will begin to curl and the flowers will wilt.

Press the plant life: Following the Microfleur instruction manual, place the botanicals between the press's two liners, top with the wool pad, and close the press. Microwave in intervals until the plant material feels dry, with the consistency of tissue paper; start checking at 40 seconds, carefully peeling and stretching the bottom liner to unstick the flowers. If they are still damp, microwave again in 10-second intervals (no longer). It is important not to overdo it here, as the flowers will continue to firm up after being microwaved. Too much time can cause the petals and leaves to burn. (Alternatively, if you're using something other than a Microfleur press, follow the manufacturer's instructions.)

Prepare the cards: Once you have assembled a repertoire of dried flowers and leaves, start to paint the front of the note cards. Choose a watercolor for the background of each card and make a wash using the flat brush on the card, working in long, wide strokes to cover the surface completely. Let dry.

Adorn the cards: Once the cards are dry, decide where to place the pressed leaves and flowers on each card's front. It's best to keep the designs fairly simple without overlapping. Using the round brush, spread the matte glue over the surface, taking care to avoid getting the very sticky glue on your hands,

if possible. Affix the botanicals to each card in the desired position and coat the entire top side delicately with more glue. Clean your brushes with warm water *immediately* after use, to keep the glue from hardening on them.

Dry the cards: If you need to hold down a petal or stem while the glue dries, slip one or more large paper clips over the item. Let the cards dry for a day. If they need further flattening, place them under a heavy book for another 12 hours or so before storing or sending.

PART VI

HIBERNAL

COME LATE NOVEMBER, THE GARDEN IS PUT TO bed for the remainder of the calendar year and for the first several weeks of the new one. While plants and animals outdoors experience the hibernal season, my daily activity moves almost entirely indoors to the studio and greenhouse. To be honest, I'm thankful for the respite, particularly once dahlia season has passed. It can be a challenge to keep pace when the flowers are in full bloom (a very lucky problem to have, I'm aware). The joy I experienced in the cutting garden just several weeks earlier gives way to the happiness of safely tucking away the dahlia tubers until next May.

The quiet garden allows me time to gear up for the cycle that will begin again after a few short, dark months. I can observe my garden structures unadorned, in their functional layout, without the leaves and flowers that camouflage everything in the growing seasons. I take note of where a fence or raised bed needs to be mended and how the metal pyramid rose supports are faring (or not, in which case I arrange for repair).

This period of dormancy is as vital to the garden as all five other periods—without it, the growing seasons would not be possible. Before long, a few hellebores make their presence known and I know that the prevernal season is soon to follow.

Holiday Flowers

Amaryllis, Paperwhite, Cyclamen

Few flowers are truly in bloom in the northeastern United States toward the end of the calendar year. Nevertheless, I try to stay close to the spirit of the Thanksgiving through New Year holidays by seeking out any fresh flowers that are available at retail or wholesale florists.

AMARYLLIS

To decorate the house, I buy cut amaryllis stems. The exuberant, richly colored blossoms can last for weeks in a vase, as long as you refresh the water every couple of days and cut the stems shorter to keep them happy. Oftentimes their stem ends form awkwardly into curlicues in vases, so trimming definitely extends their vase life. I arrange them with greens and foliage, including evergreen magnolia branches, rose hips, and foraged berry branches.

Amaryllis bulbs are available loose or already potted in late fall and, depending on when they are planted, can flower well into the winter months. I am always behind on potting my bulbs, so my amaryllis blossoms begin to open in March, just as winter's cold begins to warm into spring. Though it's later than I originally intend, it is lovely to watch them open, and they cheer me while I wait for fresh growth in the garden. I have had some success keeping amaryllis bulbs over the summer and repotting them the following year: In July, I cut the spent stems off and place the bulbs in a paper bag, which I store in a dark, cool closet or basement until November. Yet and still, I buy new amaryllis bulbs every year, too, because I find them so hard to resist. I like to order them from Van Engelen or pick up bulbs from the nice selection at Terrain in nearby Westport.

PAPERWHITE

I love the scent of paperwhites, though some people find it too strong. (Some cultivars smell sweeter than others; you can find descriptions of each in sellers' catalogs, such as that of Brent & Becky's Bulbs, page 280.) The bulbs are available at the same moment as amaryllis and are incredibly easy to force. Placed in a bowl or terra-cotta pot with potting soil or stones, they will happily bloom in a relatively short time, from four to six weeks. I usually place a small branch in the pot when I plant the bulbs; as the stems grow tall and begin to flop, they can be tied to the branch for support.

In a footed marbleized bowl, cut amaryllis flowers and winterberry and eucalyptus branches form a beautiful base for the taller burgundy calla lilies, red-and-white parrot tulips, mauve lilies, and white anemones.

(Fallen branches in the garden are perfect for this task.) I enjoy paperwhites best in the moments just before they bloom, watching as the stems emerge from the bulb and the flower bulges out of the top. Once the paperwhite flowers have opened, I often cut the long stems off the base and use them in a flower arrangement or by themselves to perfume the room.

CYCLAMEN

I keep pots of cyclamen in colors from white to pale pink to deep fuchsia in the greenhouse during the cold season and bring the pots outside to shady areas of the garden in warmer months. Planted in terra-cotta pots or simple porcelain vases, they bloom for six to eight weeks and make a cheerful winter arrangement for the table.

Cyclamen, a genus containing around twenty species, is part of the primrose family. The plants grow from a tuber with round, patterned leaves and one flower per stem. The name derives from the Greek *kyklos*, meaning "circle," which refers to the shape of its tuber; the flower symbolizes sincere affection and long friendships. The most commonly available type is *C. persicum*. Several

perennial species, including *C. coum*, are winter hardy and can be grown outside. I have seen lovely examples of this type at Kew Gardens in London and also under an old linden tree in Lucca, Italy, growing out from the moss. Like other tubers, cyclamen should not be planted too deep in the soil; otherwise, it will not bloom.

Above: A pair of porcelain bowls—one with a celadon glaze and the other a cool white bisque—hold cyclamens in bloom. The textures of the pots work well with the variegated pattern on the leaves.

Opposite: Bright and cheerful red-and-white amaryllis, including 'Santiago', 'Ambiance', and 'Très Chic', flower in my hand-thrown terra-cotta pots. Throughout the holiday season, they are displayed in the dining room so that everyone can enjoy their vibrant presence.

DREAMING OF THE GARDEN IN BLOOM

It isn't just during the quiet, cold months that I dream about which flowers to plant in my garden beds. Rather, I'm on an unrelenting quest to keep learning and trying new ideas. Often I'm inspired to try growing a new-to-me variety I may have seen on a garden tour or read about in a book. But it's in winter that I have time to pause and assess my wish list. I focus on what I have ordered most recently, how I see the upcoming season unfolding, and which flowers in which forms (bare-root roses, perennial chrysanthemums, and, yes, new dahlia tubers) will soon start arriving in boxes on my doorstep.

As I write this in early March, winter has passed more quickly than in other years in recent memory. I have been reviewing how well things grew in the garden last season and how this year's flower selection could be improved. Once again, I will try to sow seeds early enough to plant them in the ground in mid-May. As I remind myself often, hope springs eternal, and I have the best intentions as I await the zinnias, cosmos, nigellas, and amaranths I ordered, and as I prepare to plant the incredible poppy, sweet pea, and dahlia seeds that arrived from Erin Benzakein of Floret Flower Farm.

Several activities help make this dreary weather pass faster, or so it seems. In the greenhouse, that means harvesting lemons to make marmalade. I go on the hunt for Seville oranges in supermarkets and cook several batches of these as well, taking advantage of the time that I don't have to be outside. It is very soothing to concoct these confitures, and the brightness hints at spring looming on the horizon. When in doubt, make jam.

Pelargoniums and Geraniums

One summer more than fifteen years ago, I had a pivotal moment with pelargoniums when I saw them in the window at the Olson House in Cushing, Maine. This house, now part of the Farnsworth Art Museum in nearby Rockland, was the location for Andrew Wyeth's iconic painting *Christina's World*. At the time of my visit, the house was empty of furniture, but the natural light pouring into the rooms evoked the lives lived within it in a time gone by.

On wooden shelves built into one of the kitchen windows was a grouping of bright red pelargoniums in terra-cotta pots, placed in honor of the plants Wyeth painted while he visited the family (the original plants were long gone). I was incredibly moved by this connection to history. The house was in a state of disrepair (though now it is in the process of being restored) with peeling wallpapers and paint, and vines from outside growing through the door cracks. I inquired last year at the Olson House about the potted flowers and learned that the plants have since been removed, as the conservators worried that their moisture was damaging the wooden window shelves.

I have been growing pelargoniums ever since. Each spring, I plant specialty scented-leaf varieties, including mint, apple, lemon, and rose, in the garden beds outside. I plant the more accessible geraniums—the zonal geraniums—in large pots on the tennis court; you can purchase these types from any local plant nursery or home center.

Pelargoniums are often confused with geraniums, but the two are not the same. Geraniums are perennials, and pelargoniums are annuals that I bring into the greenhouse for the dormant season. Pelargoniums (and geraniums) love warmth and full sun. I wait until the soil in the flowerpots is dry and then water deeply. I add a couple tablespoons of organic liquid plant fertilizer to the watering can to encourage flower development. If a geranium isn't flowering well, it might need repotting into a larger vessel or a sunnier spot in which to grow. Pelargoniums and

I strive to maintain pelargoniums and geraniums in a variety of colors and forms in the greenhouse. One winter morning, I brought these into the studio to photograph and keep by my pottery wheel.

FAVORITE PELARGONIUM VARIETIES

Pelargonium domesticum **'African Queen'** A pelargonium with deep red flowers that have darker red splotches on the inner petals

P. sidoides South African (or African) geranium, with tiny reddish-black, butterfly-shaped flowers and rounded, ruffled blue-gray leaves

P. **'Brown's Butterfly'** A pelargonium that features almost-black flowers with velvety ruffled petals

P. **'Bernice Ladroot'** A variety with peachy-orange petals that are darker in the center, named for a longtime member of the International Geranium Society

Wood Stove, Andrew
Wyeth, 1962.

geranium plants do well with regular
pruning, so I take care to remove dead
leaves and spent flower heads. If I want
to increase my stock, I cut off the top of
a stem and place it in a glass of water to
root. After the roots sprout and grow a
few inches (6 to 8 cm), I place the new
plant in a terra-cotta pot with fresh,
organic potting soil.

I display the flowers alone in a bud
vase or combine them with tulips,
zinnias, dahlias, or whatever else happens
to be in bloom in the garden or the
greenhouse. Sometimes I keep the lower
leaves on the stems and place them at the
bottom of a vase to support other stems
in the arrangement.

After photographing a group of potted geraniums in the
window at the Olson House in Maine years ago, I was
inspired to grow many varieties myself.

ROSE GERANIUM POUND CAKE

There is nothing better than a lovely slice of pound cake with coffee at breakfast or for afternoon tea with friends. I took a classic recipe from King Arthur Baking and tweaked it by using rose-scented geranium (*Pelargonium graveolens*) leaves to flavor the sugar and to adorn the top and bottom of the loaf. This edible herb offers nicely subtle flavor and fragrance, but you could use any number of other scented geranium leaves in its place, such as apple, mint, or lemon. *Serves 6 to 8*

½ pound (225 g) salted butter, at room temperature (see Note), plus more for greasing the pan
8 rose-scented geranium leaves
1 cup (200 g) granulated sugar
2 cups (240 g) all-purpose flour
1½ teaspoons baking powder
½ teaspoon salt

4 large eggs, at room temperature
½ cup (120 ml) milk, at room temperature
1 tablespoon brandy, sherry, rum, or the liqueur of your choice (optional)
1 teaspoon pure vanilla extract, almond extract, or a combination
Sanding sugar, for sprinkling

Note: If you use unsalted butter, increase the salt in the recipe to 1 teaspoon.

Preheat the oven to 350°F (175°C).

Lightly grease a 9-by-5-inch (23 by 13 cm) loaf pan. Line the bottom and short sides with a piece of parchment paper to make a sling. Lay 3 of the geranium leaves at the bottom of the sling.

In a medium bowl, combine the granulated sugar and 2 geranium leaves. Rub the sugar and leaves together thoroughly before removing and discarding the leaves.

In a separate bowl, whisk together the flour, baking powder, and salt.

In a large bowl, beat the butter with an electric mixer on medium speed until smooth, about 3 minutes. Gradually add the flavored sugar and beat until smooth, then add the eggs, one at a time, scraping the bottom and sides of the bowl as needed and beating until the mixture is light and fluffy, 3 to 5 minutes.

In a small bowl, whisk together the milk, brandy, and vanilla.

Using the mixer on low speed, add the flour mixture and the milk mixture to the bowl with the butter, working in batches and beginning and ending with the flour. Beat just until smooth and no streaks of flour remain.

Transfer the batter to the prepared pan, on top of the geranium leaves. Lay the remaining 3 leaves across the top of the batter and sprinkle evenly with sanding sugar.

Bake the cake until it springs back when pressed lightly on top and a cake tester inserted into the center comes out clean, 55 to 60 minutes. Start checking for doneness after 40 to 45 minutes; if the cake is browning too quickly, tent it with foil for the final 15 minutes of baking. It's better to slightly undercook the cake than let it bake too long.

Transfer the cake to a wire rack and loosen the edges with an offset spatula. After 5 minutes, carefully lift the cake from the pan using the paper sling. Place it on the rack to cool completely.

The cake can be wrapped in plastic and stored for a day or two before serving, or frozen for a few months.

Greenhouse Flowers

Camellia, Begonia, Citrus Trees

About six years ago, after many years of dreaming, plotting, and planning, I had the good fortune to add a greenhouse at the base of my ceramics studio. Before that time, I spent many hours dragging potted plants into the house or studio once frost descended upon the garden. I had talked to several friends who had built greenhouses and they recommended Arcadia GlassHouse in Ohio. The installation crew showed up with a trailer and built the greenhouse in situ. They were wonderful to work with.

During the winter months, the greenhouse holds the citrus trees as well as the chrysanthemums (page 210), pelargoniums and geraniums (page 245), and auriculas (page 55). If I've potted up spring bulbs in late October and left them outside for their chilling period until about mid-January (or six weeks from potting), they are brought into the greenhouse to start the sprouting. I also keep camellias and begonias in the greenhouse year-round here.

I use organic aphid traps from the company Arbico Organics to prevent pests in the greenhouse as much as I can. I keep the greenhouse at 50°F (10°C) night and day and use a fan to continuously circulate the air in the room. When the sun is shining and the temperature outside rises, I open the door to let in air to refresh the plants.

Keeping everything alive and happy is a challenge, but it is nice to have plants that flower at different times, no matter how delicate the bloom. These plants would live well in the house, too, but I like to keep them together in the greenhouse, where I am sure to water them consistently and keep an eye on the soil, handle any necessary fertilizing, and monitor the amount of sunlight they get.

CAMELLIA

A beautiful 'Pink Perfection' camellia bush flowers in the greenhouse from January to mid-February. I purchased it a few years ago from a local nursery, and as it has grown and stretched since then, I have moved it into larger pots. When the delicate pink flowers appear, I treasure each one. I take care not to overwater the camellia (this is especially

Not every floral arrangement has to be abundant to be impactful, as is the case with this 'Pink Perfection' camellia branch displayed in an oribe-glazed, wood-fired pot.

After the greenhouse was built, it was quickly crammed with citrus trees, chrysanthemums, pelargoniums, begonias, and auriculas.

Truthfully, I wouldn't have it any other way, as the chaos allows for the abundance of flowers and plant life that I'm able to grow and arrange.

important indoors) and to keep the bush by the greenhouse door, where it gets the most sun. I fertilize it with a specialty acidic blend formulated for camellias, azaleas, and rhododendrons. According to Nuccio's Nurseries, a California-based grower of rare camellias, the plants should be fertilized—sparingly—once the buds start to form. So far, the bush is doing well. Some camellia varieties can be planted outside, depending on the growing zone, and next spring I intend to plant a suitable one against a stone wall over by the hydrangea tree, which should provide protection from the wind.

BEGONIA

Begonia flowers are pretty, but I love the leaves most. A small group of potted begonias sit together in the least sunny area of the greenhouse. Begonias are easy to grow in pots with good potting soil, in a room with east–west, preferably indirect, light (though some varieties can handle the sun). I keep them snug in their clay pots, without too much

room around the roots, and take care not to overwater—the soil should be dry to the touch before they receive water again. Even if they wilt because I haven't watered them sufficiently, I find that they come back. During the spring growing season, I add liquid organic plant fertilizer (FoxFarm Big Bloom liquid concentrate) to my watering can to keep the begonias nicely fed.

CITRUS TREES

Since I got the greenhouse, I have been collecting citrus trees. Now I grow Meyer lemons, calamondins, Buddha's hands (a type of citron), kumquats, and yuzu, and I'm always up for adding more uncommon citrus varieties. Citrus trees should be watered moderately and fertilized every month (I use Espoma Citrus-tone organic fertilizer). To give the roots room to spread, I move the trees into larger pots as needed, adding new soil each time. During the most recent winter, when some of the trees were infected by a type of scale, I laboriously wiped each leaf with an organic horticultural spray to bring the disease under control, and I rely on aphid traps (see page 275) to help me keep the plants healthy through winter. The citrus trees go back outside in mid-May, when nighttime temperatures consistently stay above 50°F (10°C). The bees love the citrus blossoms, and their fragrance is heavenly.

FAVORITE BEGONIA VARIETIES

Begonia maculata 'Wightii' Wonderfully playful white polka dot markings on green elongated leaves

B. 'Cherry Sparkle' A rhizomatous hybrid boasting deep purple-black leaves with red veining

B. 'Raspberry Swirl' A striking rex hybrid with large silver leaves swirled with hot pink and burgundy

B. 'Ribbon Candy' A rex hybrid with spiral leaves with bands of green and burgundy

I cut branches of lemons in the greenhouse and arranged their stems in a tea-dust glazed wood-fired pitcher before they were brought into the kitchen. The leaves were so fresh and green and the fruit smelled heavenly.

Orchids

In the dormant months, I seek out beautiful orchids to transplant into my terra-cotta pots. They are widely accessible these days, and look so elegant and graceful throughout the house, where I use them to decorate our Thanksgiving table every November. Their blooms can last for months. (I put several in the studio as well.)

A couple of years ago, the New York Botanical Garden had a fantastic orchid show called *Natural Heritage*, in which they exhibited the flowers as they would live in their native surroundings. (Yes, it was hot and humid in the exhibit.) I was especially enchanted by *Paphiopedilum* Valime 'Val', *Cattlianthe* Gold Digger 'Orchid Jungle', and *Paphiopedilum* 'Euryatica'. I am fortunate to live near a wonderful grower, J&L Orchids, but you can find nice orchids in all kinds of specialty stores and even at supermarkets like Trader Joe's.

I don't profess to be an expert on orchid care, and each type has its own requirements. (You can read about the different varieties on the American Orchid Society's excellent website.) However, there are a few commonalities to keep in mind, mainly taking care not to overwater them. A good rule of thumb is to place the pot in the sink once a week and water the plant deeply enough to soak the soil, then let it drain before returning the pot to its location, which should not be in direct sunlight. You can also spritz the plants from time to time (once a week is a good guideline), to mimic the humid subtropical conditions to which they are accustomed. I use an organic orchid fertilizer to keep them well fed, following the instructions on the package. Admittedly, it can be a challenge to keep these beauties healthy and thriving, but that is part of the allure of cultivating them.

Below: This jumble of orchids in the greenhouse includes *Paphiopedilum* I-Hsin 'Sesame' and a *P. amabilis* hybrid in the foreground, with a few chrysanthemums growing nearby.

Two exquisite orchids—a delicate Maudiae hybrid *Paphiopedilum* slipper orchid in a terra-cotta pot and another known as *Paphiopedilum* I-Hsin 'Strawberry Milkshake' in a stoneware vase—catch the late-winter afternoon light in the studio.

Opposite: I planted a number of *Phalaenopsis amabilis* hybrid orchids in this oblong white earthenware footed bowl and then covered their roots with moss from the tennis court garden. As long as they're kept out of the sun, the beauties will bloom for weeks, even months.

Right: A green complex or "bulldog" *Paphiopedilum* slipper orchid sits in a cobalt blue painted porcelain bowl. I love the jaunty expression of the flower and the angle of the leaves.

BEST PRACTICES FOR BUYING FLOWERS

My original intent for the garden was to allow myself access to a steady supply of flowers for the photographs that I use to help sell my pottery. In those days, I couldn't easily get fresh blooms beyond what was available in a small number of local outlets, and the pickings were often slim. Thankfully, the opportunity to purchase quality cut flowers has expanded enormously since then.

I buy cut flowers straight from the greenhouses of local growers, and from the wholesale flower market near my home in Connecticut, which is more focused on American-grown flowers of late. I make a point to steer toward these blooms.

Supermarkets, delis, and specialty food stores carry more diverse cut flowers and potted bulbs than they used to. Even if the selection is not as deep as at a wholesale flower market, the push to buy from national growers has improved. Farmers' markets that run all winter usually have some greenhouse-grown options to offer in the earliest spring.

If I need flowers for a specific occasion, I plan accordingly in order to allow time for them to be in peak condition on that date. When I bring the flowers home, I immediately remove any plastic wrapping, rubber bands, or paper. (I have noticed that plastic wrapping is used less and less, fortunately.) I trim the ends of the stems (except for the Icelandic poppies, which I do not touch) and place them in buckets tall enough to support their height, away from sunny windows. Regular tap water works just fine, and there's no need for floral preservatives, in my experience.

Cut flowers open at different times, depending on the variety. Tulips, for example, can take days to evolve into their best arranging state, depending on the temperature in the room. My studio is kept at a cool temperature—50°F (10°C) at night in winter—so flowers take longer to open in that space than they would if kept in the house, which is generally 65° to 70°F (18° to 21°C). In summer, I keep buckets in the barn basement, where the temperature is always cooler than outside. If you live in a warm climate, the flowers will, of course, open more quickly and you would have to experiment with the timing component.

I try not to select flowers that have a short lifespan, such as hellebores or violets, unless I plan to use them immediately for the dinner table or photography. Roses, lilies, daffodils, hyacinths, stocks, Japanese anemones, ranunculus, tulips, and Icelandic poppies all have a wonderful senescence, and I can use them repeatedly in photography or in the house through their various stages.

GROWING YOUR OWN

MANY PEOPLE DREAM OF GROWING FLOWERS.
Yet they struggle to get started, worrying that they lack the
expertise or the resources to be successful in their endeavors.
The truth is, anyone can learn to grow flowers, and the best way
to start a garden is simply to get started.

Over the years, I've managed to eke out as much growing
space as I can from the land that surrounds my home. No
matter your setup, there's a very good chance you can cultivate
some kind of flower wherever you are—whether within
highly designed perennial borders, from seeds carefully sown
and arranged in well-ordered rows, in meadow-like fields of
wildflowers, or as a container garden with a variety of pots. My
gardens, which are planted specifically for cutting purposes, fall
somewhere between these approaches.

Keep in mind that gardening is a slow journey. Time, the
elements, and your location will all factor into the results. Even if
your vision doesn't go as planned, whatever happens will surely
have its own rewards.

An overhead view
of the tennis court
garden on an early-
June morning, when
the roses have just
started to open. The
majority of the beds
are 3 by 8 feet (1 by
2.4 m), which is a very
practical size allowing
for easy access from
either long side.

Start with these parameters as you think about what you wish to grow. Is there a sunny, open piece of land that you can work with? You must be mindful of sun, as eight hours a day in the growing season is the requirement for most sun-loving flowers. If your garden gets fewer than eight hours, you'll have to rely on plants that can thrive in partial or full shade. There's no use in putting a sun-loving plant into a shady area; it just won't grow. (Likewise, a shade lover won't thrive in full sun.) If there's not much space in the ground for planting, do you have a deck or balcony or even a window that gets good light? If you are planting in ground, you'll need to take note of the soil, which will affect the success of your gardening efforts. And finally, consider whether there are deer or other predators in your area; if so, can the garden be fenced in?

My earliest attempts at gardening were mostly unsuccessful. A steep hill surrounded our first home in Connecticut. The land featured a rock wall with a few plants—creeping jenny and alyssum—growing all over it. Neither plant interested me much, so I looked for replacements. One distinct failure involved forget-me-nots, which I love for their blue color. I pulled the blooming plants directly from the pots, roots and all, and divided them into four or five sections, then eagerly stuck each clump into the wall wherever it might fit, all while working under a hot

midday sun. The flowers were dead by the end of the day. What had I neglected to realize? For one thing, a potted, mature plant cannot be chopped up at the bloom stage; nor can it be stuck into place beneath the blazing sun without any soil preparation. And forget-me-nots were not a good choice for a rock wall, because their growing conditions don't align with that environment at all. I struggled with this garden for a few more years until I eventually found alpine plants that could thrive there. This early garden experience helped me understand how much I still needed to learn about growing flowers. Most important, it taught me that trial and error is the absolute best teaching method. Eventually, I came to enjoy correcting my own mistakes and moving forward.

In the many years hence, I have spent a lot of time observing the plants at several nearby nurseries and asking knowledgeable plantspeople about how to achieve my plant goals and adapt things to my specific environment as needed. Now I try to gather as much information as I can before I buy anything. Yet and still, some plants never manage to thrive, but I don't consider garden experimentation of any kind to be a failure, and neither should you. In fact, I encourage you to keep trying new things and chalk up any unfortunate results to your ongoing education in gardening.

Flower Growing Basics

What follows are several general guidelines for cultivating flowers. Anything specific to a particular plant is highlighted within the preceding flower profiles. The following are things to keep in mind once you've decided which flowers you wish to grow and whether you have the correct conditions, such as hours of sunlight and climate, to meet the plant's growing requirements.

I also encourage you to approach gardening (and flower arranging—see page 276) with sustainability in mind. In both endeavors, I try to stay informed of current research and best practices as much as possible.

Begin with Healthy Soil

Growing great flowers sustainably starts with healthy soil, which is made up of layers of compost, manure, organic fertilizer, sand, and lime; this provides the essential foundation for the trees, shrubs, and flowers. What adjustments your soil may need will depend on the geographic region of the garden and the particularities of your land. There are recipes for compost teas, worm castings, and biomatter that will accelerate the soil-improvement process, but the best approach is to seek the advice of plantspeople in your growing region as to what should be added to the bed if the soil is lacking a key ingredient.

I build up the humus, or decomposed plant and animal matter, in my soil year after year with leaves from the trees on our land as well as organic cow manure. The compost from the pile gets applied to the beds. It took a few seasons for the soil to

settle in, but the amendments have made all the difference in the health and longevity of the garden, which is maintained without any chemicals or other unnatural additives.

I try to turn over the beds as little as possible to avoid disturbing the worms and other organisms living in the soil, taking care to dig gently when I put plant material into the ground. I avoid synthetic fertilizers, and generally feed the plants with organic fertilizers such as fish emulsion. After the perennial plants have emerged from the ground and the dahlia tubers and annuals have been placed, I cover the beds with sterile straw to keep the weeds and unwelcome volunteers from taking over; it will eventually biodegrade and enrich the soil.

Seeds

I prefer to plant organic and heirloom seeds, seeking them out from reputable suppliers (see page 280 for some of my favorites). If you order seeds during the winter months, make a chart to remember when the packet advises you to start the seedling process.

The first step when sowing seeds is to determine whether the seed must be started indoors ahead of the growing season or if it can be directly sown in the soil. This happens once the temperature has warmed enough (in Connecticut, this is usually about mid-May, after the last frost). The process is relatively simple and straightforward, as follows:

STARTING SEEDS INDOORS

1. Determine when you need to start the seeds, based on the number of weeks the seedlings need to reach planting size as well as the proper air and soil planting temperatures outdoors.

2. Purchase an organic seed-starting mixture and small biodegradable pots (such as CowPots) that will sustainably dissolve into the garden after planting. Or you can choose a seed-starting kit, which will include a heating mat, planting trays, and covers. Either way, plan to set the pots or trays under grow lights or near a sunny window.

3. Check the seed packet to determine the depth the seeds should be planted and whether they should be lightly covered by soil.

4. Once the seeds are planted, keep the soil moist but be sure not to overwater. It's best to water the pots from below by setting them in the shallow trays filled with water and refilling as needed, so as not to disrupt the seed germination.

5. After the seeds sprout, watch for the second set of true leaves and pinch these out to encourage branching.

6. As planting time approaches, harden off the seedlings by putting the tray outside during the day and bringing it back indoors at night until the seedlings gradually acclimate to the outside temperature.

7. When the outside temperature remains about 50°F (10°C) at night, carefully pop seedlings out of the planting tray and set them into the garden bed; plants started in CowPots can go directly into the bed, pot and all.

DIRECT-SOWING SEEDS

1. Check the information on the seed packet about the best time to sow outdoors. Depending on your location, some seeds can be planted outdoors in autumn for germinating the following spring.

2. Plant the seeds at the correct depth and spacing according to the packet's instructions. To make sure I have plenty of options, I tend to put more than one seed in a hole and then move the extra seedlings around after they have sprouted.

3. Watch for sprouting and protect the seedlings with organic slug repellent pellets, a plastic cloche, and/or a deer and rabbit repellent such as Plantskydd.

4. After the first set of leaves has formed, watch for the second set of true leaves and pinch these out to encourage branching.

5. Water the garden adequately to keep the seedlings from drying out and getting stressed.

Tubers

Purchase tubers online from larger companies in the early-summer months for the best selection. The tubers will be shipped the following spring. Smaller suppliers each have their own tuber release date, and the best way to be informed is to sign up for their email newsletter. If you miss the window, however, I've found that the larger growers still have a decent selection of tubers available in spring. Wait until it is above 50°F (10°C) at night before you get started. Follow the steps below for best results when planting tubers:

1. Dig a hole relative to the size of the tuber with an inch (2.5 cm) or so around it. Older, stored tubers will be large while newly purchased ones are generally smaller.

2. Take care not to plant the tuber too deep in the soil; anything deeper than a couple of inches (5 cm) for a new tuber could cause it to rot.

3. Put in some kind of support system—a tomato cage or a stake, for example—for the tuber as it grows.

4. You don't need to water it right away; the ground is usually sufficiently moist at that time of year, and you want to take care not to drown the tuber.

Plugs

Flower farmers are now offering an excellent variety of plugs, which are starter plants grown individually in small pots that are ready to transplant. As a result, I am no longer as dedicated to growing from seed as I was years ago. Gardeners can purchase many of the rare types of flowers online in the early months of the year, and the farmer will grow the plants to order for delivery at the correct planting time (for me, that's May). I've found that beginning with larger and healthier flowers that have been hardened off (or gradually acclimated from the greenhouse to the outdoor temperatures) increases my success rate and abundance of cutting flowers. Follow the steps below when planting plugs:

1. Water the plugs thoroughly when you receive them and before pulling them out of their plastic tray.

2. Try to plant the plugs as soon as possible after purchasing. If they haven't been hardened off by the grower, do that now.

3. Pull off the bottom ½ inch (1.3 cm) of soil and roots to stimulate new root growth.

4. Pinch off the plant's top bud, flower, or second set of true leaves to encourage branching.

5. Dig a hole in the garden bed appropriate to the width and depth of the plug.

6. Water again once the plug is planted.

Planting Bulbs

Some varieties of bulbs are planted in fall, others are planted in spring. Order your fall planting bulbs (such as tulips, certain varieties of lily, daffodils, muscaris, hyacinths, and fritillaries) in late May or early June if you want the best selection; order those you'll plant in spring (like lilies, and corms such as gladioli) in the autumn months or in January. If purchasing bulbs in a bag from a store, make sure they are not dried out and shriveled. Follow these guidelines for best results:

• Each bulb requires a different planting depth and spacing. Carefully read the instructions that come with your bulbs (though I tend to plant bulbs more closely together than directed).

• It is optimum to plant the bulbs when the shipment arrives in fall, but as long as the soil is not hard frozen, there is a good window for getting them into the ground. Bulbs that are planted in spring go in when the soil is workable; for Connecticut, this is generally in mid-May.

• For tulips, dig a long trench (mine is usually about 4 inches/10 cm deep by 12 inches/30 cm wide and the length of my 16-foot/4.9 m bed). Place the bulbs a few inches (7.5 cm) apart; for fullness, I put three across each row down the length of the trench. Or, using a narrow hand trowel, dig out holes one by one and place the bulbs among existing perennials.

• Bulb fertilizer is optional; some years I use it, if I have the time, and other years I do not. If you choose to do so, be sure to sprinkle it over the bottom of the trench or put a few tablespoons in each hole.

• Restore the soil over the bulbs; there's no need to water them after planting, as any snow or rain over the long winter months will take care of that.

Forcing Bulbs

Many (but not all) bulbs are good candidates for forcing, including crocuses, muscaris, fritillaries, hyacinths, and some varieties of daffodils and tulips. The practice is a nice way to bring color and cheer indoors during the dormant days of winter, before plants start to emerge in spring. To force them, I generally put multiple bulbs cheek by jowl in a terra-cotta pot. It's not an exact science, but the following steps should help ensure a good result:

1. Place a drainage layer in the bottom of your pot (stones work well).

2. Cover with an inch or two (2.5 to 5 cm) of dirt.

3. Place netting over the dirt (to keep voles and mice out) and top that with leaves or sawdust for insulation.

4. Place the pots outside in a sheltered area, or even a cold frame, until it's time to bring them back inside to spur growth (for me, this is in mid-January or early February).

A Garden Tools Glossary

The right tool will serve you well in the garden year after year, as long as you take care to preserve it. Keep your tools clean, and importantly, bring them inside after use rather than leaving them in the elements to rust and deteriorate.

1. **Hand trowel.** A trowel comes in handy when digging holes to plant bulbs, seedlings, and plugs; having a few in a range of widths will allow you to dig holes of various sizes.

2. **Weeding tools.** The two pictured here each have pointed narrow ends, which are helpful for removing grass and weeds that have grown between the flowers without disturbing the flowering plants' roots.

3. **Japanese hori hori.** This knife can handle so many garden chores, from digging holes to trimming off branches. Attach its accompanying sheath to a garden belt for quick and continual access.

4. **Needle-nosed clippers.** These are excellent for harvesting flowers.

5. **Secateurs.** I use these Niwaki Mainichi specialty clippers on thicker branches and rosebushes.

6. **Jagged-knife tool.** This can trim thicker branches and dig small holes in the beds.

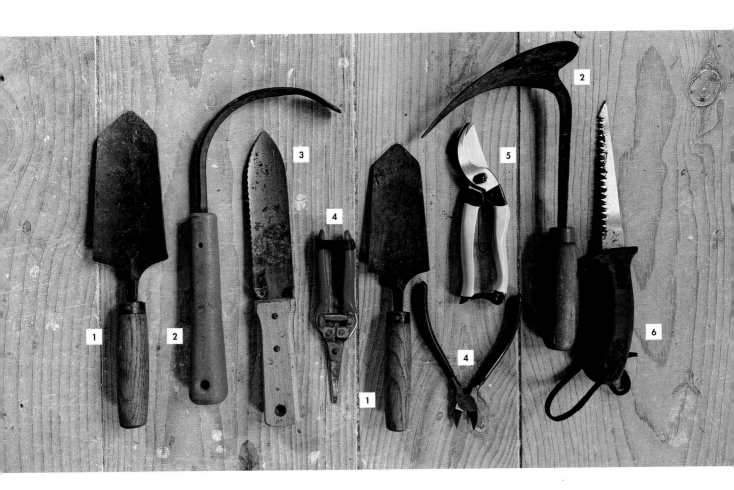

7. **Pitchfork.** This is the garden tool I reach for most frequently. I have several sizes and rely on them instead of a shovel when moving dirt aside to place a plant because they offer the added benefit of aerating the soil.

8. **Rake.** This comes in handy for cleaning away the leaves from paths in the round garden.

9. **Small shovel.** I have a good selection of Sneeboer garden tools, and this delicate shovel is nice for planting in small spaces.

10. **Large shovel.** An ideal tool for planting shrubs and small trees.

11. **Broom.** There's nothing better to help keep the tennis court surface well swept.

12. **Deep spade.** Another effective tool for planting large shrubs and small trees.

Care & Maintenance

My best advice for anyone who wants to grow flowers is to consider the relationship with the garden as an active one, from season to season. Be mindful of the needs of the plants and the soil from which they grow, which includes figuring out the best way to provide adequate water, the most effective and least harmful fertilizers, and how to protect from pests.

WATERING

For most of the years that I have had my cutting garden, I haven't needed to start watering the gardens until late May. More recently, however, weather patterns have been rapidly shifting. This year the drip irrigation was turned on mid-May, as was the overhead sprinkler in the round garden. Keep the following pointers in mind as you water your flowers:

- It is best to water in the early morning, so that the leaves and flower heads have time to dry. Watering at night increases the possibility of fungus and rot developing.

- When watering flowers or shrubs in pots, aim the hose down toward the soil and roots and not over the entire plant.

- When using drip irrigation, use the sensor mode so that the system doesn't run if there has been good rainfall. Overwatering will cause roots to rot as well as make the environment ideal for slugs and snails.

FERTILIZING

Nearly every plant that's cultivated in the garden needs help from time to time in order to thrive. That said, I've found that there are plenty of ways to provide nutrients without relying on chemical fertilizers and nonorganic amendments. Below are a few guidelines to fertilize in more sustainable ways:

- A general organic flower fertilizer such as Flower-tone or North Country Organics can be spread over the beds and around the perennials in early spring (for me, this is April) before planting annuals.

- Starting in early summer (for me, late June), use a sprayer to cover the garden with organic fish emulsion (½ cup/120 ml emulsion concentrate to 2 gallons/7.5 L water).

- In autumn, after tubers (like dahlias) have been lifted and any bulbs have been planted, this is a good time to spread a layer of an organic cow manure mulch over the garden beds to promote the health of the soil over the winter.

- Once the manure is applied but before the hard freeze, spread leaves over the beds for extra protection and to provide habitat for insects. The leaves disintegrate over winter and can be worked into the soil when annuals are planted the following spring.

PEST CONTROL

I try to use as few chemicals in the garden as possible, but there are a number of pests and predators that can be difficult to control. In many cases, you can take measures to keep them from compromising your flower garden, but in some cases, you may need to call your local animal control experts. Keep the following in mind:

- **Aphids.** To control the aphids that can appear on my plants in the greenhouse, I use two products. The first is an organic sticky insect trap from Africa Organics that catches both aphids and whiteflies. The second is a horticultural oil called neem that I dilute in water and wash over every leaf with a sponge. This is time-consuming but essential to keep the plants and citrus trees healthy while they're inside over the winter. Once they're back outside, these pest issues are usually resolved.

- **Deer and rabbits.** A fence surrounding the garden is the most effective deterrent to these animals. If this is not possible, organic animal sprays such as Plantskydd applied to foliage make plants less appealing. The only trick is to keep up the spraying, as the product gets washed off by rain or loses its effectiveness after a couple of weeks have gone by.

- **Red lily beetles.** For the most part, I grab these by hand off the plants, sometimes taking the leaf they are resting on as well, and crush them under my shoe. If I missed one and it laid eggs that develop into that awful gooey black larvae on the underside of leaves, I wear rubber gloves and wipe the larvae off the plant. This maintenance can go on for a couple of months.

- **Japanese beetles.** I walk through the garden with a jar of soapy water and wipe these off the flower into the liquid. They especially like to hide in the rose and dahlia petals, so I have to carefully search. If this strategy isn't sufficient, I spray with an organic insect repellent such as neem oil. Beetle traps are not effective in my garden, and I don't like to see them hanging off the trees.

- **Slugs.** I have used organic Sluggo or Captain Jack's slug pellets throughout the beds just as the dahlias and annuals are sprouting, because the slugs will mow down new growth overnight.

WEEDING

I find that focusing on creating healthy, organic soil and planting perennials and annuals closely together significantly cuts down on the weeds. That said, I continually go through the garden and pull out invasives, vines, and grasses that have infiltrated the beds. You can also apply a layer of sterile straw to keep the weeds down between the rows of flowers, as I do around the dahlias in the round garden. Invasive bittersweet, pokeweed, and poison ivy in particular must be kept at bay.

PRUNING

Simple pruning of dead flowers and snapped stems is easy to do with garden clippers. But for the rosebushes, apple trees, shrubs, and flowering trees, I feel it is important to hire a professional to have the pruning done correctly. If this is not in your budget, consider taking a class or studying a book on the correct way to prune. This makes all the difference in the health of the garden and long-term life of the shrub, rosebush, or tree.

Flower Arranging Basics

Though I've been working with flowers for decades, there are always new ways to approach the process, because the arrangements are never quite the same from one day to the next. Once you start to practice with flowers frequently, you can be more experimental and play around with varieties, colors, shapes, and textures.

The more you arrange flowers, the more that each bouquet doesn't feel quite so consequential. In fact, the ephemeral nature of flower arranging is precisely what makes the pursuit so appealing. No combination of flowers is permanent, so there's always a next time to build a new, wholly original arrangement.

I've found that the best way to become adept is to interact with the garden regularly. This is how you truly learn to appreciate the differences between the seemingly endless varieties of flowers. I try to arrange in the moment and look closely at how to best work with the flowers at hand, and to keep going until I feel that I've said all that I have to say.

I am also mindful of ecological concerns. In that endeavor, I have learned much from the British floral designer Shane Connolly, who describes himself as a "floral alchemist." Connolly advocates for sustainable plant materials and uses flowers sourced from local growers in his work. He has been instrumental in creating positive changes in the industry standards of the flower world. I often think about his philosophies as I cut flowers in the garden and put the stems into buckets of water without any chemical preservatives. And when I am arranging blossoms in a vase, I avoid plastic tape, plastic flower tubes, or floral foam, which are made from harmful chemicals and anathema to sustainability.

The best time of day to pick flowers is early morning. Ensure your clippers are sharp and not rusted, and cut your stems as long as possible. You never know when you might need an extra-tall stem to punctuate an arrangement at the finish.

Put the flowers in water as soon as you can after cutting; either bring a bucket of water with you out to the garden or use a flower trug and have the water waiting in the house or studio.

When choosing a vase, let the intended function of the arrangement guide you. Will it go on a dinner table or a side table? Would a widemouthed vase be best, or something with a narrower opening? Once you have the vessel and the flowers in hand, it's time to start building your bouquet. The steps opposite should serve as guidelines.

The best way to extend the life of flowers in a vase is to change the water and cut fresh ends off the bottom of the stems every few days. Remove any spent blooms and rearrange those that still look acceptable. Once the blossoms have completely faded, I transfer them to a compost pile. (Because there are usually weeds in the pile, I don't use this compost in the raised beds, but it provides a fertile growing space for volunteer native plants like goldenrod, milkweed, and aster.)

Establish the foundation by adding branches, vines, or supporting flowers to the vessel or using a flower frog to hold the blossoms in place. (The wider the mouth, the more important it is to add a support system; frogs are especially useful in bowls and widemouthed pots.) This arrangement's foundation is grounded in tiny purple asters.

Keep building out the base by adding flowers and other organic elements (such as the amaranth and coleus leaves shown) that contribute interesting colors and textures. Try not to overthink the placement of the stems.

Add a few focal-point flowers (here, dahlias and zinnias). From there, work in descending order from thickest stems and biggest heads to smaller and more delicate specimens, like the salvia, Japanese anemones, and asters in this arrangement. Move things around, starting with the less weighty flowers, and maybe remove a stem or two. If you wish to add a trailing element, place this last.

Stand back and take a wide view, making any final adjustments. When you are pleased with the arrangement, document it with your camera. Photographing is another important part of the process of getting better at arranging flowers.

Gardens to Visit

I often plan my time away around visiting gardens—new ones as well as those that I have seen before but can never seem to get enough of. What follows is a list of my favorite gardens around the world, though it could easily be much longer. By the time this book goes to print, chances are I will have added to it.

ALHAMBRA AND GENERALIFE GARDENS
Granada, Spain

These incredible gardens were formed to represent the Persian ideal of paradise, with design commencing around 1238. The fountains and plantings weave in and out of the castle perched on top of a mountain, and the sound of water is incorporated into the beautiful symmetry and complexity of the design. I am amazed by the tranquility and elegance of the garden rooms and how they are integrated with the buildings they surround.

CHANTICLEER
Wayne, Pennsylvania

The home and garden of the Rosengarten family dates to the early twentieth century and was opened to the public in 1993. The original estate consists of seven garden rooms of diverse habitats, thoughtfully holding more than five thousand different types of trees and plants. Rather than tag each individual flower, the garden's staff is on hand to help visitors with design and maintenance questions.

CHELSEA PHYSIC GARDEN
London, England

The Chelsea Physic Garden along the Thames in London was founded in 1673 by the Worshipful Societies of Apothecaries to study medicinal plants. I visit there every time I go to London. Some of the beds are planted by geographic location and some by the medicinal use of the plants. I always take notes about what is growing and what support structures are used, and then as soon as I return home, order something similar for my garden. I love the feeling of history in the place, and they have a wonderful restaurant for lunch.

THE HIGH LINE
New York, New York

The High Line is built on the abandoned 1½-mile (2.4 km) elevated freight rail on the west side of Manhattan. It was conceived as a park in 1999, and the first stage opened to the public in 2009. The structural element was designed by Diller Scofidio + Renfro, and the landscape design is by Piet Oudolf. As the years have gone by, the maturation of native species and trees has been a wonder. I love to walk through the park from the subway at Thirty-Fourth Street down to the Whitney Museum of American Art at Gansevoort Street. Every season has a different display and provides all sorts of ideas for pollinator planting.

LES JARDINS DE QUATRE-VENTS
La Malbaie, Quebec, Canada

This is not the easiest garden to reach, but it's well worth the effort to secure a ticket on the annual Open Day. Designed and carefully overseen by the late Francis Cabot, an important American garden preservationist and the founder of the Garden Conservancy, the 20-acre (8 ha) estate features more than twenty-five diverse types of gardens. My favorite areas are the Japanese teahouse, the Pigeonnier with the dramatic pool, and the beautifully sited Moon Bridge.

NEW YORK BOTANICAL GARDEN
Bronx, New York

This historical gem of a garden was founded in 1891 and is a museum of living plant collections. Spread over 250 acres (101 ha), it has something blooming at all times of the year. I especially look forward to the annual orchid exhibition in the Enid A. Haupt Conservatory; the Mertz Library is home to brilliant botanical and painting exhibitions.

ROUSHAM HOUSE & GARDENS
Oxfordshire, England

Rousham is an estate built in 1635 for Sir Robert Dormer and still owned by his family. The centuries-old design feels incredibly contemporary and relevant today. What truly drives me crazy (in the best way) is the small, concrete-rimmed stream, or rill, that snakes through the landscape and ends at a small pool surrounded by trees. Its design cannot be improved upon, and it continually inspires my work, as I aim to keep my forms streamlined, refined, and gracefully crafted. Rousham also has three seventeenth-century walled gardens that give me many ideas about which flowers to plant and how to combine them for a dense and vibrant effect, especially the extravaganza of foxgloves around the pigeon house and the herbaceous borders filled with roses, gorgeous perennials, annuals, and espaliered fruit trees.

SAIHOJI/KOKEDERA (MOSS TEMPLE)
Kyoto, Japan

Before being allowed to wander the Saihoji Temple garden, originally opened in 1339, visitors enter the monastery building for an initiation ceremony of writing calligraphy on paper. After this exercise, they are permitted to enter the garden to contemplate its beauty. The ancient moss and trees are truly a wonder, and a sense of timelessness pervades.

SAKONNET GARDEN
Little Compton, Rhode Island

Described by its owners, John Gwynne and Mikel Folcarelli, as "a secret garden embedded within a native coastal landscape," Sakonnet was private for many years but is now open to the public. I highly recommend a visit to see the gardeners' most magical, unexpected plantings inside beautiful garden rooms divided by stone walls.

SISSINGHURST CASTLE GARDEN
Kent, England

This British garden has a long and storied history. The famous garden that one can visit today was originally created by Harold Nicolson and Vita Sackville-West when they purchased the property in 1930. Sackville-West often wrote about her bold ideas, such as her garden room comprised of only white flowers, and what she was planting throughout the property. Its design has been the inspiration for many flower-loving gardeners in the years since. It is truly a place that can be visited at any time of the growing season.

WAVE HILL
Bronx, New York

This public garden is designed at the most wonderful scale. Formerly a private estate, the landscape along the Hudson River features different garden areas that invite contemplation and provide an education about plantings.

Go-To Suppliers

Here are the growers and purveyors I rely on most, and the plants, seeds, pots, and tools that I get from each—but many carry much more than what is listed. Visit their websites to see the bounty of beautiful offerings for yourself.

FLOWERS

Adelman Peony Gardens
Salem, OR
peonyparadise.com
Peonies

Ambler Farm
Wilton, CT
amblerfarm.org
Amaranths, marigolds, sunflowers, and zinnias

Baker Creek Heirloom Seeds
Mansfield, MO
rareseeds.com
Coreopsis, nigellas, poppy seeds, and sunflowers

Barnhaven Primroses
Plestin-les-Grèves, France
barnhaven.com
Auriculas

Bluestone Perennials
Madison, OH
bluestoneperennials.com
Chrysanthemums and Japanese anemones

Brent & Becky's Bulbs
Gloucester, VA
brentandbeckysbulbs.com
Dahlias, fritillaries, gladioli, lilies, and tulips

Broken Arrow Nursery
Hamden, CT
brokenarrownursery.com
Dogwoods, lilacs, and viburnums

The Bunker Farm
Dummerston, VT
thebunkerfarm.com
Hard-to-find annuals including delphiniums, poppies, salvias, and zinnias

Cricket Hill Garden
Thomaston, CT
treepeony.com
Fruit trees and peonies

David Austin Roses
Tyler, TX (and the UK)
davidaustinroses.com
Roses

Eden Brothers
Arden, NC
edenbrothers.com
Dahlias and lilies

Fast Growing Trees
Fort Mill, SC
fast-growing-trees.com
Citrus trees

Ferncliff Gardens
British Columbia, Canada
ferncliffgardens.com
Dahlias

Floret Flower Farm
Mount Vernon, WA
floretflowers.com
Zinnias, celosias, and dahlia seeds

Geraniaceae
Kentfield, CA
geraniaceae.com
Geraniums and pelargoniums

Heirloom Roses
St. Paul, OR
heirloomroses.com
Roses

High Country Roses
Broomfield, CO
highcountryroses.com
Roses

Honker Flats
Middle River, MN
honkerflats.com
Gladioli

Issima
Little Compton, RI
issimaworks.com
Asters and pollinators of all kinds

J&L Orchids
Easton, CT
jlorchids.com
Orchids

Johnny's Selected Seeds
Fairfield, ME
johnnyseeds.com
Marigolds, sunflowers, sweet peas, tulips, and zinnias

King's Mums
Oregon City, OR
kingsmums.com
Chrysanthemums

K. van Bourgondien
Lawrenceburg, IN
dutchbulbs.com
Dahlias

McClure & Zimmerman
Randolph, WI
jungseed.com
Lilies

Menagerie Farm & Flower
Live Oak, CA
menagerieflower.com
Roses

Monrovia
Locations throughout the US
monrovia.com
Azaleas

The Shop at Monticello
Charlottesville, VA
monticelloshop.org
Historic seeds, including hyacinth bean

Nagel Glads
Milwaukee, WI
nagelglads.com
Gladioli

Nuccio's Nurseries
Altadena, CA
nucciosnurseries.com
Camellias

Old House Gardens
Ann Arbor, MI
oldhousegardens.com
Dahlias, gladioli, hyacinths, and tulips

Oliver Nurseries
Fairfield, CT
olivernurseries.com
Azaleas, dogwoods, rudbeckias, witch hazels, and viburnums

Pine Knot Farms
Clarksville, VA
pineknotfarms.com
Hellebores

Renee's Garden Seeds
Felton, CA
reneesgarden.com
Zinnias

Schreiner's Iris Gardens
Salem, OR
schreinersgardens.com
Irises

Sequim Rare Plants
Sequim, WA
sequimrareplants.com
Auriculas

Spring Hill Nursery
Tip City, OH
springhillnursery.com
Lilacs

Swan Island Dahlias
Canby, OR
dahlias.com
Dahlias

Terrain
Glen Mills, Devon, and Doylestown, PA; Westport, CT
shopterrain.com
Amaryllis bulbs

Thompson & Morgan
Ipswich, England
thompson-morgan.com
Amaranths and sweet peas

Van Engelen
Bantam, CT
vanengelen.com
Amaryllis bulbs, fritillaries, lilies, and tulips

White Flower Farm
Morris, CT
whiteflowerfarm.com
Azaleas, bleeding hearts, clematis, delphiniums, hydrangeas, lilacs, and lilies of the valley

FLOWERPOTS

Ben Wolff Pottery
Goshen, CT
benwolffpottery.com
Classic, hand-thrown flowerpots

Campo de' Fiori
Sheffield, MA
campodefiori.com
Classically designed pots

Snug Harbor Farm
Kennebunk, ME
snugharborfarm.com
Wonderful terra-cotta pots designed by Tony Elliott

GARDEN TOOLS

Felco
Seattle, WA
america.felco.com
High-quality clippers and pruners

Gardenheir
Windham, NY
gardenheir.com
Traditional and excellent-quality garden tools—I like Niwaki brand

Garden Tool Company
gardentoolcompany.com
Shovels and trowels for digging plants

Further Reading

The Art of Arranging Flowers by Constance Spry
The original flower arranger's timeless ideas on how to think about flowers.

Floret Farm's A Year in Flowers: Designing Gorgeous Arrangements for Every Season by Erin Benzakein with Jill Jorgensen and Julie Chai
A thorough and gorgeous guide to growing, cutting, and arranging.

A Flower Garden for Pollinators by Rachel de Thame
A primer on attracting pollinators, with charming illustrations by the author's daughter.

The Flower Hunter: Seasonal Flowers Inspired by Nature and Gathered from the Garden by Lucy Hunter
Inspired by the landscape, with wonderful visual inspiration and a romantic, natural approach to flowers.

Martha's Flowers: A Practical Guide to Growing, Gathering, and Enjoying by Martha Stewart with Kevin Sharkey
A beautifully illustrated, authoritative guide to growing and arranging flowers throughout the seasons, using the bounty from Stewart's gardens.

Mastering the Art of Flower Gardening: A Gardener's Guide to Growing Flowers, from Today's Favorites to Unusual Varieties by Matt Mattus
A very useful, flower-by-flower guide to growing in great detail.

On Flowers: Lessons from an Accidental Florist by Amy Merrick
A beautiful and clever way of looking at flowers and how to work with them in an array of vessels.

Some Flowers by Vita Sackville-West
Originally published in 1937 and reissued in 2014, featuring essays by the legendary British gardener on her twenty-five favorite flowers, with illustrations by Graham Rust.

The Tulip Garden: Growing and Collecting Species, Rare and Annual Varieties by Polly Nicholson
A thorough exploration of tulips, both historical and contemporary, including which ones to choose and how to grow them.

Uprooted: A Gardener Reflects on Beginning Again by Page Dickey
A delightful chronicle of the author's transformation of her church house garden into a new iteration of native and natural plantings.

A Way to Garden: A Hands-On Primer for Every Season by Margaret Roach
The first book that taught me how to plant and maintain flowers, and a great primer on how to garden sustainably.

Wild Colour: How to Make and Use Natural Dyes by Jenny Dean
Clearly explained techniques for making natural dyes for yarns and textiles.

A Year in Bloom: Flowering Bulbs for Every Season by Lucy Bellamy
A fantastic survey of bulbs, both lesser and the most well-known.

A Year in Flowers: Inspiration for Everyday Living by Shane Connolly
Photographs of his exquisite seasonal arrangements, and suggestions for how to approach flowers in a sustainable way.

Acknowledgments

I would like to acknowledge the following people for their help in producing my second foray, *Life with Flowers*. It has been an exciting process.

Thank you to my family: Wallace, Daphne, David and Wyeth, Martina and Cooper, Ethan and Megan, and granddaughters arriving soon.

To Ellen Morrissey, without whom I could not have made this book. I am grateful for your expertise both textual and visual. Your contribution on all matters was essential.

To Carla Glasser, my agent and sounding board. I value your friendship and professional guidance.

To Lia Ronnen, for asking me to write this book as a companion to *Life in the Studio*.

Thank you to Bridget Monroe Itkin, my editor at Artisan, who has guided this project with great insight and style.

Thank you to Erin Benzakein for graciously writing the foreword. I admire your amazing expertise with your flowers, business, and life.

Thank you to my assistant, Kim Risolo, who helps me with everything and listens to me!

Thank you to Jane Treuhaft and Elizabeth Van Itallie for your book design and Nancy Murray for production and attention to color.

Thank you also to everyone at Artisan who has helped with book production: Laura Cherkas and Hillary Leary, Paula Brisco, Abby Knudsen, Suet Chong, Zach Greenwald, Theresa Collier, Allison McGeehon, and Moira Kerrigan.

Thank you to Rebecca Stepler for help with photography permissions.

Thank you to Johanna Pfund and Kate Caprari, who manage my beautiful website and overall design.

Thank you to the photographers who have contributed the additional images: Michael Biondo, Dean Hearne, Peden + Munk, Helen O'Donnell, Jane Beiles, and Weston Wells.

Thank you to David Wagner for your photographic technical expertise.

Thank you to Grace Kennedy, Marilyn Young, Laura Mulligan, Sarina Vetterli, Consuelo Quesada, Christina Koether, Cathy Deutsch, Taylor Johnston, Ed Bowen, Eileen O'Connor, and Page Dickey for your advice and help in the garden. Thank you to Derick Cockburn for maintaining the fruit orchard.

Thank you to King's Mums, Schreiner's Gardens, J&L Orchids, and Issima for your help with identifying plants. Thank you to Jacob Moss and East Coast Wholesale Flowers as well.

Thank you to Abby Bangser for your friendship and for being a part of Object & Thing.

Thank you to Megumi Shauna Arai and Kiva Lopez Motnyk for your guidance on the marigold dye project.

Thank you to Dominique Browning, Susan Morgenthau, Melissa Ozawa, Stephen Orr, Anne Hardy, Charlie McCormick, Ben Pentreath, Phoebe Cole Smith, David Wilson, David Hopkins, Amy Merrick, Marion Brenner, Leslie Giuliani, Zizi Mueller, Dale and Jamie Gould, Shane Connolly, and Laurie Hawkinson for your support and friendship.

Index

Page numbers in *italics* indicate photos.

ageratum, *216,* 221

Albers, Josef, 232

Alhambra and Generalife Gardens, 278

allium, 137–138, *139, 149*

amaranths, 224, *225–227*

amaryllis, 236, *237, 238, 241*

annuals, 18

  ageratum, *216*

  amaranths, 224, *225–227*

  borage, 144, *146,* 148, *149, 150,* 151

  calendula, 144, *146,* 151, 180, *181*

  dill, 144, *144–146, 149*

  flowering vines and climbers, 120

  hyacinth bean, *122,* 123, *218–219*

  larkspur, *139,* 143

  marigold, *149, 178,* 179, 180, *181, 182,* 183, *184–185,* 185

  morning glory, *122,* 126, *218–219*

  nasturtium, *122,* 126–128, *129*

  nigella, 142, *150*

  pelargoniums, *244,* 245

  poppies, *114,* 115, *116–119*

  salvia, *216,* 217

  snapdragon, *139,* 142–143

  sunflowers, 164, *165–167,* 166, 220

  sweet pea, *122,* 127

  verbena, *146,* 148

  zinnias, *186–189,* 187–188

anthotypes, *74,* 75–76, 77

apple tree blossoms, *38*

apricot tree blossoms, *38*

asters, *218–219,* 222, 223

Atkins, Anna, *70,* 71

auriculas, *54, 55,* 55–56, *57, 254*

autumnal period, 197

azaleas, *82–85,* 83

bearded iris, 23, *86–89,* 87, *90–91, 91*

bee balm, *216,* 220

begonia, *254,* 255

Bell, Vanessa, 21, *21*

Benton End, 23, *23*

biennials

  foxglove, *136,* 138, *139,* 141, *150*

  hollyhock, *136, 139, 140,* 143

  verbascum, *136,* 137, *139, 150*

bleeding hearts, *98,* 99, *99*

blossoming fruit trees, *38,* 40

borage, 144, *146,* 148, *149, 150*

Bouquet of Flowers, 71, *71*

bulbs/corms

  allium, 137–138, *149*

  amaryllis, 236, *237, 238, 241*

  crocus, 29, 30, *30, 31*

  daffodils, 44, *45–46,* 47

  fritillaries, *32,* 33, *34–35*

  gladioli, *158,* 159–160, *161*

  hyacinths, *50–51,* 51–52, *53*

  lilies, 48, *130–133,* 131, 134, *135*

  muscaris, *42–43,* 43

  paperwhite, 236, *238,* 239, *239*

  planting or forcing, 271

  snowdrops, *28,* 29, 29–30

  tulips, 64, *64–66,* 67–69, *68, 69*

buying flowers, 262

Cabot, Francis, 141, 279

calendula, 144, *146,* 151, 180, *181*

camellia, 250, *251,* 255

Camera Work (Steichen), 72

Carroll, Lewis, 14

A Celebration of Clematis (Heafey), 124

Chanticleer, 213, 278

Charleston, 21, *21*

Chelsea Physic Garden, 120, 278

Chez Panisse Menu Cookbook (Waters), 152

Children, John George, 71

chives, *146,* 148, 151–153, *153*

Christina's World (Wyeth), 245

Christmas rose, 26

chrysanthemums, 210, *211–212,* 213

citrus trees, *253,* 255, *256–257*

clematis, *122,* 123–124, *150*

climbers, flowering. *See* flowering vines and climbers

coleus, 191–192, *193*

Connolly, Shane, 48, 276

Corbin, Pan, 111

cosmos, 176, *177*

crocus, 29, 30, *30, 31*

"Cromer's Amateur," 71, *71*

cup and saucer vine, 120, *121, 122,* 123

cutting gardens, 14–15, *16–19,* 18

cyanotypes, *70,* 71

cyclamen, 239, *240*

daffodils, 44, *45–46,* 47

dahlias, 48, *198–199,* 199–200, *201–205,* 206, *207*

Delany, Mary, 55, *55*

delphinium, *139,* 141–142

Delphiniums (Steichen), *73*

Deutsch, Cathy, 40

Dickey, Page, 40, 137, 163

dill, 144, *144–146, 149*

Diller Scofidio + Renfro, 278

Discovering the Meaning of Flowers (Connolly), 48

dogwoods, 92, *92, 93*

Dormer, Robert, 279

early-flowering branches, 36, *37–38,* 39–40, *41*

  apple tree blossoms, *38*

  apricot tree blossoms, *38*

  blossoming fruit trees, *38,* 40

  forsythia, *38,* 39

  magnolia, *38,* 39–40, *41*

  pussy willow, 36, *38*

  redbud, *38,* 40

  witch hazel, 36, *37, 38,* 39

East Anglia School of Painting and Drawing, 23

echinaceas, 170, *170–172, 173*
Egeskov Castle, 159
elderflower, *146,* 151
Elliott, Tony, 124

ferns, *193–195, 195*
fertilizing, 274
feverfew, 144, *146,* 147, *150*
Fibonacci, Leonardo Pisano, 164
fig leaves, 192, *193*
Finnis, Valerie, 43
flower growers, 163
Flower-Topped Sugar Cookies, 62, *63*
flowering herbs, 144, *144–146,* 147–148, *149, 150,* 151–153, *153*
  borage, 144, *146,* 148, *149, 150*
  calendula, 144, *146,* 151, 180, *181*
  chives, *146,* 148, 151–153, *153*
  dill, 144, *144–146, 149*
  elderflower, *146,* 151
  feverfew, 144, *146,* 147, *150*
  lavender, 144, *146,* 147
  sage, *146,* 147, *149*
  verbena, *146,* 148
flowering shrubs or trees, 18
  apple tree blossoms, *38*
  apricot tree blossoms, *38*
  azaleas, *82–85, 83*
  blossoming fruit trees, 40
  camellia, 250, *251,* 255
  dogwoods, 92, *92, 93*
  early-flowering branches, 36, *37–38, 39–40, 41*
  elderflower, 151
  forsythia, *38,* 39
  hydrangeas, 156, *157*
  lilacs, *60,* 61
  magnolia, *38,* 39–40, *41*
  pussy willow, 36, *38*
  redbud, *38,* 40
  roses, 48, 102, *103–106,* 107–108, *108–109,* 111, *162,* 163

viburniums, 92, *94,* 95, *95*
witch hazel, 36, *37, 38,* 39
flowering vines and climbers, 120, *121–122,* 123–124, *124–125,* 126–128, *129*
  clematis, *122,* 123–124, *150*
  cup and saucer vine, 120, *121, 122,* 123
  hyacinth bean, *122,* 123
  morning glory, *122,* 126, *218–219*
  nasturtium, *122,* 126–128, *129*
  passionflower, *122,* 124, *124–125,* 126
  sweet pea, *122,* 127
Folcarelli, Mikel, 26, 279
forsythia, *38,* 39
foxglove, *136,* 138, *139,* 141, *150*
Friedlander, Lee, 69, *69*
fritillaries, *32,* 33, *34–35*
fruit trees
  blossoming, *38,* 40
  citrus, *253,* 255, *256–257*

Garden People (Finnis), 43
Garrett, Fergus, 22
geraniums, *244,* 245–246, *247,* 248–249, *249*
gifts, flowers as, 48, *49*
gladioli, *158,* 159–160, *161*
Gladstar, Rosemary, 169
goldenrod, 214, *215, 216,* 217, *218–219*
Grant, Duncan, 21
grape leaves, 192, *193*
Great Dixter Charitable Trust, *20,* 21, *21,* 22
greenhouse flowers, 250, *251–254,* 255, *256–257*
  begonia, *254,* 255
  camellia, 250, *251,* 255
  citrus trees, *253,* 255, *256–257*
Grounded in Clay, 11–12
growing flowers, 265–266, *267,* 268–275, *272, 273*

bulbs, 271
  care and maintenance, 274–275
  plugs, 270
  seeds, 268–269
  soil, 268
  tools for, *272, 272–273, 273*
  tubers, 270
Gwynne, John, 26, 279

Hadspen, 137
Halibut with Chives in Parchment, 152–153, *153*
Hammershøi, Vilhelm, 51, *52*
Haverman, Margareta, 64, *64*
Heafey, Kaye, 123, 124
helianthus, *216,* 220–221
hellebores, 26, *27*
herbs, flowering. *See* flowering herbs
Herschel, John Frederick William, 71, 75
hibernal period, 235
The High Line, 278
holiday flowers, 236, *237–241,* 239
  amaryllis, 236, *237, 238, 241*
  cyclamen, 239, *240*
  paperwhite, 236, *238,* 239, *239*
hollyhock, *136, 139, 140,* 143
Hortus Bulborum, 51, 64
hosta, 192, *193*
hyacinth bean, *122,* 123, *218–219*
hyacinths, *50–51,* 51–52, *53*
hydrangeas, 156, *157*
hyssop, *216,* 221

Interior Strandgade 30 (Hammershøi), *52*
iris, 48. *See also* bearded iris
Iris (Jones), *72*
Iris Seedlings (Morris), 23, *87*

Japanese anemone, *218–219,* 228, *228–231*
Japanese maple, *190,* 191, *193*
Jefferson, Thomas, 123
Joe-pye weed, *216,* 220

Jones, Charles, 72, *72*
Joséphine, 102

Kazumasa, Ogawa, 131, *131*
Kertész, André, 68, *69*
kirengeshoma, 192, *193*, 195

larkspur, *139*, 143
lavender, 144, *146*, 147
leaves (foliage), *190*, 191–192, *193–195*, 195
  coleus, 191–192, *193*
  ferns, *193–195*, 195
  fig leaves, 192, *193*
  grape leaves, 192, *193*
  hosta, 192, *193*
  Japanese maple, *190*, 191, *193*
  kirengeshoma, 192, *193*, 195
  smoke bush, *193*, 195
  Solomon's seal, *193*, 195
lemon verbena, *146*, 148
Lenten rose, 26
Lentil Salad with Nasturtiums, 128, *129*
Les Jardins de Quatre-Vents, 141, 279
Lett-Haines, Arthur, 23
Liggett, Larry, 56
lilacs, *60*, 61
lilies, 48, *130–133*, 131, 134, *135*
lilies of the valley, 96, *96–97*
Lily (Kazumasa), 131, *131*
Linnaeus, Carl, 170, 173
Lloyd, Christopher, 21, 22
Love-in-a-mist, *139*
Lutyens, Edwin, 21

magnolia, *38*, 39–40, *41*
Manet, Édouard, 79
marigold, *149*, *178*, 179, 180, *181*, *182*, 183, *184–185*, 185
marigold-dyed napkins, *182*, 183, *184–185*, 185
Mattus, Matt, 141
Melancholic Tulip (Kertész), 68, *69*

milkweed, *216*, 217, 220
Modotti, Tina, 102
Moench, Conrad, 170
Monardes, Nicolás, 220
morning glory, *122*, 126, *218–219*
Morris, Cedric, 22–23, *23*, *87*, 90
mountain mint, *218–219*
muscaris, *42–43*, 43

nasturtium, *122*, 126–128, *129*
natural order of plants, 12
New City, New York (Friedlander), *69*
New York Botanical Garden, 55, 199, 210, 258, 279
Nicolson, Harold, 279
nigella, 142, *150*

Old Fashioned Flowers (Sitwell), 56
orchids, 258, *258–261*
Oudolf, Piet, 278

paperwhite, 236, *238*, 239, *239*
passionflower, *122*, 124, *124–125*, 126
pelargoniums, *244*, 245
peonies, *78*, 79–80, *81*
Peonies (Manet), 79
perennials, 18
  ageratum, *216*, 221
  asters, *218–219*, 222, 223
  auriculas, *54*, *55*, 55–56, *57*, *254*
  bee balm, *216*, 220
  begonia, *254*, 255
  bleeding hearts, *98*, 99, *99*
  chives, 148, 151
  chrysanthemums, 210, *211–212*, 213
  clematis, *122*, 123–124, *150*
  cosmos, 176, *177*
  delphinium, *139*, 141–142
  echinaceas, 170, *170–172*, 173
  feverfew, 144, *146*, 147
  flowering vines and climbers, 120
  geraniums, *244*, 245–246, *247*, 248–249, *249*

goldenrod, 214, *215*, *216*, 217, *218–219*
helianthus, *216*, 220–221
hellebores, 26, *27*
hollyhock, *136*, *139*, *140*, 143
hyssop, *216*, 221
Japanese anemone, *218–219*, 228, *228–231*
Joe-pye weed, *216*, 220
lavender, 144
milkweed, *216*, 217, 220
orchids, 258, *258–261*
passionflower, *122*, 124, *124–125*, 126
peonies, *78*, 79–80, *81*
poppies, *114*, 115, *116–119*
rudbeckias, 170, *172–175*, 173
sage, *146*, 147, *149*
sunflowers, 164, *165–167*, 166, 220
verbascum, *136*, 137, *139*, *150*
verbena, *146*, 148
vernonia, *216*, 221
personas of flowers, 14
pest control, 100, 275
photographing flowers, 18, *70–73*, *71–72*
Photographs of British Algae (Atkins), 71
planting plan, 15, 18
plugs, 270
poisonous/toxic plants
  foxglove, *136*, 138, *139*, 141, *150*
  hellebores, 26, *27*
  hyacinth bean, *122*, 123, *218–219*
  hyacinths, *50–51*, 51–52, *53*
  larkspur, *139*, 143
  lilies of the valley, 96, *96–97*
  milkweed, *216*, 217, 220
pollinator species, 18, 214, *215*, *216*, 217, *218–219*, 220–221
  ageratum, *216*, 221
  bee balm, *216*, 220
  goldenrod, 214, *215*, *216*, 217, *218–219*

helianthus, *216, 220–221*
hyssop, *216,* 221
Joe-pye weed, *216, 220*
milkweed, *216,* 217, 220
salvia, *216,* 217
vernonia, *216,* 221
Polypodium Phegopteris (Atkins), *70*
poppies, *114,* 115, *116–119*
pottery, 11–12, *13. See also individual photos*
pressed-flower cards, 232–233, *233*
prevernal period, 25
pruning, 275
pussy willow, 36, *38*

Queen Anne's lace, *218–219*
Quesada, Connie, 107
Quince Jelly with Rose Petals, *110,* 111

recipes
  Flower-Topped Sugar Cookies, 62, *63*
  Halibut with Chives in Parchment, 152–153, *153*
  Lentil Salad with Nasturtiums, 128, *129*
  Quince Jelly with Rose Petals, *110,* 111
  Risotto with Fresh Flowers, 180, *181*
  Rose Geranium Pound Cake, 248–249, *249*
redbud, *38,* 40
rhizomes
  bearded irises, *86–89,* 87, *90–91, 91*
  lilies of the valley, 96, *96–97*
  sunflowers, 220
Risotto with Fresh Flowers, 180, *181*
River Cottage Preserves Handbook (Corbin), 111
Roach, Margaret, 39
Rose Geranium Pound Cake, 248–249, *249*
roses, 48, 102, *103–106,* 107–108, *108–109,* 111, *162,* 163

Rousham House & Gardens, 138, 279
Rudbeck, Olof, 173
rudbeckias, 170, *172–175,* 173

Sackville-West, Vita, 279
sage, *146,* 147, *149*
Sakonnet Garden, 26, 279
salvia, *216,* 217
Schell, Bosco, 163
seeds, 268–269
serotinal period, 155
Sheeler, Charles, 187, *187*
shrubs. *See* flowering shrubs or trees
Sissinghurst Castle Garden, 56, 137, 279
Sitwell, Sacheverell, 56
smoke bush, *193,* 195
snapdragon, *139,* 142–143
snowdrops, *28, 29,* 29–30
Soijoji/Kokedera (Moss Temple), 279
soil, 268
Solomon's seal, *193,* 195
Some Japanese Flowers (Kazumasa), 131
Somerville, Mary, 75
spires, *136,* 137–138, *139, 140,* 141–143
  allium, 137–138, *139, 149*
  delphinium, *139,* 141–142
  foxglove, *136,* 138, *139,* 141, *150*
  hollyhock, *136, 139, 140,* 143
  larkspur, *139,* 143
  nigella, 142, *150*
  snapdragon, *139,* 142–143
  verbascum, *136,* 137, *139, 150*
Spry, Constance, 22, *22*
Steichen, Edward, 72, *73,* 102, 141
Steiner, Rudolf, 100
Stieglitz, Alfred, 72
sunflowers, 164, *165–167,* 166, 220
suppliers, 280–281
sweet pea, *122,* 127
symbolic meanings of flowers, 48

Talbot, William Henry Fox, 232
talking to flowers, 14
Tate Gallery, 23
Tenniel, Sir John, *14*
Through the Looking-Glass (Carroll), 14, *14*
tools, *272,* 272–273, *273*
trees
  blossoming, *38 (See also* flowering shrubs or trees)
  citrus, *253,* 255, *256–257*
tubers
  cyclamen, 239, *240*
  dahlias, 48, *198–199,* 199–200, *201–205,* 206, *207*
  growing, 270
tulips, 64, *64–66,* 67–69, *68, 69*

A Vase of Flowers (Haverman), 64, *64*
Venison, Tony, *23*
verbascum, *136,* 137, *139, 150*
verbena, *146,* 148
Verey, Rosemary, 142
vernal period, 59
Vernon, William, 221
vernonia, *216,* 221
viburniums, 92, *94,* 95, *95*
vines, flowering. *See* flowering vines and climbers

watering, 274
Waters, Alice, 152
Wave Hill, 39, 279
A Way to Garden (Roach), 39
weeding, 275
witch hazel, 36, *37, 38,* 39
Wood Stove (Wyeth), *246*
Worshipful Societies of Apothecaries, 278
Wyeth, Andrew, 245, *246*

Zinnia and Nasturtium Leaves (Sheeler), 187, *187*
zinnias, *186–189,* 187–188